Kept
WOMEN

Kept
WOMEN

Confessions from a Life of Luxury

LESLIE McRAY
with Ted Schwarz

WILLIAM MORROW AND COMPANY, INC.
New York

306.735
McR

Library of Congress Cataloging-in-Publication Data

McRay, Leslie.
    Kept women / Leslie McRay with Ted Schwarz.
       p.   cm.
    ISBN 0-688-08021-9
    1. Mistresses—Psychology. I. Schwarz, Ted, 1945–
II. Title.
HQ806.M37   1990
306.73'5—dc20

89-12706
CIP

Printed in the United States of America

First Edition

1 2 3 4 5 6 7 8 9 10

BOOK DESIGN BY KATHRYN PARISE

I dedicate this book to Greg Bautzer
who was responsible for getting me addicted
and unaddicted to the "kept" life-style.

———————

PREFACE

I never wanted to write this book. Even now, as Ted Schwarz and I complete this volume, I am frightened by what I am doing.

I am forty-three years old. I have traveled throughout the world. I have dined with political and business leaders. I have known top entertainers. I have appeared on the covers of magazines, been desired for my beauty, been told that I am the object of other women's envy, of men's desires. Yet inside I am a scared child, desperate for a father's approval I will never have, wanting a mother's love when both she and I are afraid to speak freely to each other.

I started this book for many reasons, perhaps the most honest being that I had hit bottom in my life. I had run from relationship to relationship, wanting to be admired, to be feted, to know that there would be someone to care for me, be concerned about my comfort, want me to have the best of everything. I told myself I was basking in adoration I truly deserved, yet in reality I was avoiding commitment. The men I knew, the great movers and shakers of the world, were shallow when it came to their relationships. They could make decisions that would better the lives or endanger the survival of millions, but, in their own way, they were also scared little boys who needed a beautiful woman to make them feel young, make them feel potent, make them feel special.

The men who kept me over the years were "dancers." We would waltz around life, avoiding such obstacles as caring, sharing, exposing our souls. And when each of us knew too much about the other, when the veil of fantasy was lifted from our eyes, even for a second, I raced to find a new man before the old one could find a new woman. We both needed our illusions, and interrupting the waltz could mean facing the lack of depth that was our lives.

As I grew older I maintained the façade of the sophisticated woman, counselor and friend to others, knowledgeable, beautiful, intelligent, the grande dame in the game of life. Yet I was actually a cutthroat competitor, living in terror that I was becoming too old, too unappealing, too familiar with the players I needed to maintain the illusions.

And then it happened. I was too old. At a time when a woman is just beginning to hit her prime, when she is physically and emotionally mature, seasoned by enough of the joy and sorrow that life brings to us all, her face filled with the richness of experience that is the true mark of beauty, I saw myself a failure. I could no longer play the game. I had to look in the mirror and see someone I did not understand, was not certain I wanted to know.

The telephone still rang, of course. There were still offers to go to Monaco, to Greece, to Paris. But the offers were different from before. The men were obviously shallow, their desires so base that I could no longer carry on the lie.

But who was I, this glamorous, formerly kept woman who was suddenly wondering if life was worth continuing? And who were the others, my sisters in glamour and pain, who occasionally grace the pages of magazines such as *Town & Country, People, Elle, Time, Newsweek,* and so many others? Why had we become what we were? What else could we be? And what hope was there for our future?

I decided that no matter what emotional hell might be involved, I had to find out the truth about not just myself but about kept women in general. I contacted author Ted Schwarz and, together and apart, we began interviewing kept women, psychiatrists, psychologists, and others. We asked them questions in what we hoped would be a nonthreatening manner that would make them comfortable revealing some layer of their personalities. Instead, we found that the kept women were remarkably candid, almost desperate in their desires to reveal all. They told us the most intimate details of their childhoods, of their relationships, their sex lives, their hopes, their fears, and the reasons they were either in the life or trying to get out of it. The only request that they made was that they and the men who kept them be left anonymous.

Thus throughout this book the names of the women we interviewed have been changed at their request; only the quotes and the case histories are factual. In addition, a number of therapists we interviewed requested that they remain anonymous so that they could provide specific patient information without violating the patient confidentiality. Any relation between the names used in place of those of our interview subjects and any women or men not interviewed for the book is strictly coincidental.

The following are the results of our research, the sometimes glamorous, sometimes titillating, sometimes tragic, and always fascinating world of the kept woman. I remain scared, even now that the book is complete, because I still fight to lead a normal life from day to day. I am trying to use my newfound understanding to move forward, to recognize that each new day brings the start of what can be the best years of my life. I am learning to love, to be vulnerable, to accept pain and pleasure, to recognize that I have value even though I have always sought my sense of worth in the reactions of others.

In part I am seeking understanding, both by and for myself. In part, I am hoping to reveal the tragic reality behind a world that gives the façade of being the ideal life-style a woman can enjoy. And in part, I am hoping to reach other young women who still have a choice in what they do and how they live.

Yet no matter what you may feel when you have finished with this book, please know that it is the most accurate, intimate, and totally revealing look into the lives of kept women ever undertaken. You may be shocked more than you ever imagined possible. You may find yourself fascinated by a secret world that few are both privileged enough and damned enough to enter. But when you are done, you will leave my world with an understanding it has taken me half a lifetime to achieve.

Leslie McRay

ACKNOWLEDGMENTS

Special Thanks:
   I would like to thank all the women who so generously shared and bared their souls as well as their innermost secrets for this book. They have all requested that they remain anonymous. I love you all. Without God I could never have survived to write about this hidden subject matter. Thank you to the support of my family.

   Too, thanks to USA Business Computer of Canoga Park, California, for its assistance. This book could not have been completed under the conditions required without its Turbo/XT model and in-house back-up support.

CONTENTS

INTRODUCTION

"Wanted: Young (21–30), attractive, slim, outgoing, child-less, intelligent lady, nonsmoker, nondrinker, animal lover, to act as a constant companion to financially well-off, non-marriage-minded bachelor. Rewards: Tax-free compensation $25,000 per year. All benefits: clothing, jewelry, residing on a small estate, traveling the world. Winters in California. If you would like to live out your dreams, send letter and full-front photo."—Classified advertisement in the Cleveland Personals section of *Cleveland* magazine.

So far as anyone could tell, Tina Barron was one of the luckiest women in Beverly Hills. She lived in an expensive apartment with her husband, Rudolfo, a man who regularly traveled throughout the world on business. She drove a Rolls-Royce convertible, had lunch at the trendiest restaurants, worked out regularly in a health club where membership fees exceeded the incomes of most of the employees, and was seldom seen wearing the same dress twice. "A woman of breeding," her friends explained. "Educated out East somewhere." "Comes from a moneyed family, I think." "Met Rudolfo in Cannes, Monte Carlo, one of those places." "A typical example of wealth marrying wealth."

Jane Higgins led a slightly different life-style. Everyone knew her background because her friends had worked with her in the public relations firm where she started as a receptionist and worked her way up to being an account executive. "It made us sad when she quit," said a former co-worker in the Chicago agency. "I mean, she seemed perfectly happy here. She was making a good living, at least forty thousand dollars with the accounts she had, but I guess she came into some money somewhere. Parents dying or something like that. She was always a little vague and we didn't want to hurt her by prying. It must have been awfully painful for her, even though they did leave her well off. She has a nice apartment, nothing fancy but certainly more than any of us could afford at the agency. Her car is a new one, too. A Buick or something. Nice, you know? She says she's free-lancing a bit

15

to keep her hand in, but that inheritance must have been something. Quitting the agency and all. It must have been something."

What none of their friends realized was that Tina Barron and Jane Higgins had more in common than the fact that both women were no longer in the workplace. Rudolfo Barron was not Tina's husband, though she agreed to use his last name. And Jane Higgins had not received an inheritance. Tina, Jane, and dozens of other women like them are kept women. They are women who have left the workplace, the singles bars, and more conventional relationships in order to be fully or partially supported by a man they will never marry.

"I once figured out that I earn a thousand dollars a day in cash and benefits from Rudolfo," said Tina Barron. "A thousand a day. Now you tell me, what person is going to be offered that kind of money and still stay in the job market? Why should I work? Why should I worry about being trained for anything? I make more than the CEOs of most corporations and I don't even have a high school diploma. I earned my GED when I was twenty-seven because I was embarrassed by not having it. But beyond that, I'm fit only to wait tables, look pretty behind a receptionist's desk while answering telephones, or do some other boring job. I'd have to go to college, then get in a profession and work my tail off, and maybe not get anywhere even then. This way I have it all, and can you honestly tell me that you wouldn't do the same thing if you could?"

Jane Higgins's experience is somewhat different. She is being kept by one of her former clients, a man who runs a midsize corporation and found he wanted to spend more time with Jane than he could in her office. He jokingly told her that it was cheaper to put her up in an apartment, give her a car, and pay her a salary that was higher than her potential at the agency than to pay the bills he would receive if he monopolized her time during working hours. " 'So make me an offer I can't refuse,' I told him," said Jane. "And he did. He pays my room, board, and taxes, so to speak, and I'm free to do anything I want so long as I'm available to him when he wants me. I'm working on that great American novel we all talk about when PR people get together, though we know none of us will ever do it. And I'm free-lancing for some of the local magazines that would probably want a story about me rather than by me if they knew. Maybe I won't get anywhere with any of that, but why should I care? I was working for security I never felt I had, and now I'm not working and have that security. Odd, isn't it?"

Tina and Jane are kept women, individuals whose life-styles are often the envy of other women who fantasize what it would be like to have a man want to pay their bills, buy them presents, and shower them with wealth while asking little in return. But who are these women? What are their lives like? And where do they find the men who keep them? The answers that were discovered during the course of researching this book are surprising.

1

Power, Sex, and the Women Who Play to Win

To be a kept woman is to participate in a game of power and control where the players are often the most admired and envied individuals in the world, with their faces gracing the covers of *Time, Newsweek, People, Paris Match, Stern,* and numerous other international publications. The clothing the players wear determines the styles followed by millions of others throughout the world. The cars they buy, the places they party, where they live all establish for others what are considered the most desirable life-styles achievable on the face of this planet. They are the objects of our collective fantasies, the people who do what others only dream about, no matter how sensual, costly, violent, or obscene. They counter indulgence in rich food by going to spas costing more per day than the average worker may make in a month. They counter inclement winter by jetting to wherever the sun is shining, even if that location is halfway around the world. And they counter the moral restrictions of society with well-placed bribes, carefully orchestrated violence, and, when it best serves their self-interest, murder.

The male players must have money, influence, or fame, coupled with a fear of commitment, of aging, of losing whatever they have that they value the most. The women must be beautiful, intelligent, and pliant to the point where they have been so carefully broken in spirit that they will completely debase themselves while thinking that they are in control. The two sexes have a love-hate relationship which few ever admit to. They are symbiotic beings engaged in a dance of such subtle complexity that each partner both leads and follows without ever being certain when the switch is made.

The female players call themselves "kept women" when they have the courage or insight to put a label on their personal life-styles and actions. They are usually young, because being older is not desirable. Women in their twenties say that they are too old for the competition they once dominated. Women in their forties say that their peak was passed at twenty-four. And women in their fifties are either no longer playing the game, perhaps married to men who were the highest bidders for their well-preserved but overly used bodies, or easing their emotional pain through alcoholism, drug addiction, or suicide.

The women are seen in expensive cars they could never afford themselves. They hostess parties in mansions that are their "homes" only so long as they please the men who pay the mortgages. They travel the world on someone else's gold or platinum American Express Card. And in the dark, where they are called upon to perform the otherwise unspoken erotic fantasies of the men who keep them, they will do anything that allows them to spend another night, another week, another month, or another year living a life-style that is simultaneously seductive and destructive.

"The first night I met him, he said, 'How would you like to spend the next year of your life traveling the world with me? I have to go to Greece tomorrow. We could start then.' I hadn't had a date with him yet. I was young, beautiful, and fit his fantasy. That was what he wanted—a fantasy. He had no idea what I was like other than my appearance. That was what he wanted to buy."

Allison

"We have to be better in bed than other women, more creative. We have to drain him dry and have him begging for more. It's a control over him."

Naomi

"My gimmick was that I wouldn't sleep with them. I said no and it intrigued them. It kept them coming back to me."

Janelle

"He was crude, violent. The first time we were intimate, he pushed me to my knees and said, 'Unzip my pants, take it out, and get me off, bitch!' It was then that I thought he was in love with me. He had taken me to a fabulous restaurant where the meal cost more than I was making in a week on my job. He had driven me to his place in a Rolls-Royce. And there he was telling me exactly what he wanted from me sexually. All other men I had been with just took me. They forced me to have sex whether I wanted it or not. They were angry if I couldn't anticipate their fantasies, which, of course, no one could. This man treated me with dignity in public and told me exactly what sex acts he wanted me to perform when we were alone. It was such an improvement, I stayed with him, taking the emotional abuse for the next three years.

Frances

The term "kept women" is one that is controversial, even among the women who are kept. "It's the pussy business," said one noted observer of the rich and famous, a writer who had once been kept herself. "There's no difference between kept women and the Beverly Hills or Fifth Avenue women who married their husbands to benefit from their money, power, and influence. They have rings on their fingers and public respectability, but don't let them kid you. They sold themselves to the highest bidder who could offer them the greatest prestige."

"They're not whores," said a two-hundred-dollar-an-hour call girl who frequently is paid to travel with men to the same destinations as kept women are—Las Vegas, Monte Carlo, Paris, Rome. "I'm independent. I choose my men carefully, I dress well, I'm intelligent [she has a bachelor's degree in mass communications and a master's degree in business administration], and I can pass for someone who's been born to royalty. But I don't have any illusions. I'm making a mid-six-figure income right now and I can walk away tomorrow. I've got real estate I own, stock investments, some rare coins and antiques. I'll retire when I can't compete anymore and I'll get into something else. No one will know what I did because I'm planning to move to the Midwest, set up my own business, and maybe marry some square john who will never know how I earned my living.

"The kept women aren't like me. They get gifts and some of them keep them. But most of them don't care about that. They're totally dependent on the man for approval. They're terrified that they're going to be rejected. They're not in business. They're living a neurotic fantasy on a scale that's like some television soap opera of the wealthy. I don't want anything to do with them."

A third woman, currently kept by an Asian whose ancestry is from a royal family, said, "I deserve the best. I'm beautiful. I'm intelligent. If a man wants to buy me fancy clothing, give me presents, take me to expensive restaurants, and put me up in an apartment, why shouldn't I let him? I deserve it. I deserve it all. I'm special and I'm not going out with someone who doesn't recognize that fact."

Would she marry the man, who happens to be single, if he proposed to her? "Sure, so long as he continues to keep me in the same style."

But do you love him? she was asked. What if he lost all his wealth and power?

"I don't know," she admitted. "I've worked in my life. I've worked hard and I've had to go hungry at times. Maybe if the troubles were short-term and I could see that the future would be better . . . I'm a good cook. I can make great meals at home. We don't have to go to a restaurant.

"Things would have to get better, though. Why should I live with a loser?"

But if you love him?

"What does love have to do with it? I'm special. I deserve the best."

The third woman's attitude was typical of the attitude of many of the kept women who were interviewed. At first glimpse, it seems an attitude of vanity and conceit reinforced, in some instances, by the fact that they are beautiful, intelligent, and seemingly special. Yet their statements often belie a subconscious reality few admit until they are older. The exaggerated sense of self-worth many express publicly often hides tremendous insecurity and fear. These are women who frequently have an intense dislike for themselves. At some time in their childhoods, many have felt themselves rejected by a strong adult male figure, usually their father, and they are subconsciously terrified of further rejection. They are also desperate for male approval, which comes through being given gifts, being made to feel important at an elaborate party, being sexually desired, especially if the man is married. To not be kept means, to them, that they are as worthless as they feel. They take no pride in their personal accomplishments, which often are worthy of great respect. They have been so psychologically abused as children that they can not view themselves positively.

Their lack of self-worth is even more surprising when you look at the backgrounds of many of the kept women. Almost all the kept women we interviewed for this book have had high-income, glamorous, and/or responsible positions. Their backgrounds include being a top model, a bank executive, a professional magazine photographer published internationally, a talent-booking agent, a producer of trade shows, a motion picture producer, a real estate executive, a syndicated columnist, a successful author, an insurance underwriter, and a commercial pilot, among others. Most of their incomes ranged from thirty thousand dollars to high six-digit figures. Yet their accomplishments don't matter to them; it is only through being kept that many feel a sense of identity.

Perhaps the greatest problem the kept woman faces is the seductiveness of the life-style. So long as the woman has her youth and her looks, the world is literally hers. She can be exposed to experiences that are more exciting than any seen in movies.

For example, once Janelle entered the life-style, she had an experience that she was desperate to duplicate ever after. The head of a nation decided that he wanted to keep her.

Janelle's experience took place in Monte Carlo, one of the most glamorous areas of the world, a city that is a hedonist's delight, with its crystalline beaches and rich blue water. It is also a working city for models and photographers who use it as a backdrop to sell fashions, cosmetics, and other items that are either expensive or meant to give the image of success.

As Janelle explains: "My flight from California was long and tiring, the hotel room I was provided, pleasant but small. My modeling agency had acted as the go-between for a new client who wanted to consider using me for some secret project. I was told that I would be contacted after I arrived, that I was to go to the hotel and wait.

"Since I was experienced in the business, I thought I knew what to expect. Whenever a new product line was being introduced, especially in the highly competitive cosmetics field, millions of dollars might be spent on the launch. Everything was always kept secret so competition would not know what was happening. I expected that I would be examined by someone from this unnamed company, then either sent back to the States or hired for an immediate photo session. The location might be exotic but the work would be that old familiar grind.

"When I answered the knock at my hotel door, a gray-haired man in shorts, sandals, and a print shirt was standing there. 'Janelle?' he asked.

" 'Yes,' I said.

" 'Good. I've come to look at your book.' He pushed past me, noticing my figure in the robe I was wearing.

"The reality of modeling is that, at times, we are just so much meat. We are measured and poked, our faces studied, our hair checked, and we are generally treated like a fine race horse being placed at auction. It is nothing personal, a fact that seems simultaneously reassuring and insulting. Yet it made me accept what happened next with this stranger.

"First the man looked through my book, a portfolio of photographs, advertising tear sheets, and covers. The best of my professional life was carefully displayed to show my versatility, my looks, and my potential for other work.

"Then he began touching me, running his hand through my hair, adjusting my robe for slightly more cleavage, checking my legs. 'Very good,' he said. 'Excellent. The report I received about you was correct.'

"The 'report' apparently related to a preliminary interview I had had in Manhattan. It had taken place in a midtown office building with men who were obviously from the Middle East. It had also been arranged through my modeling agency and they had never explained the potential job.

" 'You will join my family and me for dinner at our villa on the ocean,' he said. 'My secretary will be your date. I want to observe you further.' Then, as an afterthought, he said 'You may call me Riza.'

"The name meant nothing to me and the idea of dinner with the family did not impress me. I could not tell if I was going to get a job or an all-expenses-paid vacation. The way he had touched me had obvious sexual overtones, yet that had happened with other men. It was the price of being in the business; something to which you learned not to respond so they would back off.

"That night was interesting but uneventful. I was picked up in a limousine, riding with the secretary who was to be my 'date,' with Riza sitting in back. He obviously expected me to be interested in him but was creating an illusion for his family.

"I suspected his wife was aware of the deception, but I couldn't help playing naïve. I began holding the arm of the male secretary, kissing his cheek occasionally, whispering in his ear. It was as though I found the man fascinating and could not take my eyes off him. Naturally the secretary was both embarrassed and delighted. He knew that he was to be the front for Riza, yet here was a beautiful woman seemingly enamored with him upon first meeting. His face seemed to be blushing all evening; Riza was irate but unable to say anything.

"It was toward the end of the week that Riza informed me that I had, indeed, been auditioning for a job. He was looking for a woman who would become the spokesperson for Iran. The woman, who had to be beautiful and intelligent, would travel with the shah throughout the world. She would represent the Iranian people to the Americans, their most important ally. Previously a beautiful blond model from Texas had held this post, but she left after six years. If I would accept, I would take her place.

"The offer was intriguing. According to Riza, if I worked for the shah, I would want for nothing. I would have a house back in the States for myself, another house for my parents, and, of course, housing, food, clothing, and other things in Iran. I would be well paid and either hold the job for life or have severance pay when I left, the amount enabling me to never have to work again. Although it was never said, the implication was that I would also serve as the shah's mistress.

"I didn't know where Riza fit in the government, but it was obvious that he lived extremely well. I could believe that the shah would be generous and the offer was extremely tempting. However, I explained how hard I had worked to reach my level of success as a model. The idea of stopping before I had seen how far I could go did not appeal to me. I wanted to continue working, not leave everything to work for a foreign country.

"Riza only smiled. He told me of a party being held in my honor on Saturday night that he felt would change my mind. What he did not say was that it would prove to be the most exciting experience of my life, a seduction by wealth and power greater than I had previously witnessed.

"For the next few days, Riza and I were together regularly. We went to the beach to sunbathe. We dined at expensive restaurants. We enjoyed the sights of Monte Carlo away from his wife and children. Always he was respectful, yet always he was touching, encouraging my response, seeing how far I would go. Even if I had been interested, I would have held back. He was the advance man for the shah, or so I assumed, and I had the feeling that how I acted would be related to his employer.

"It was on a Friday that a designer and two seamstresses came to my hotel door. I had been moved from my original quarters to a suite of rooms, where they took over the living area in order to prepare a gown for the next night's affair.

"There is a trick to being a kept woman that I had already learned. Although I was not interested in meeting the shah, I did want to please Riza in the same manner I pleased the men who kept me over the years. To do this I had to dress in a manner that would hold his attention without upsetting the other women.

"The fabrics I was shown were extremely expensive. The one I chose, a flesh-colored, almost see-through silk, would have cost hundreds of dollars a yard to purchase. It had a paisley print that was large, sheer, and barely visible. On my body, it would be revealing enough to be seductive yet conservative enough to not be embarrassing.

"The gown was to have full-length sleeves, billowing at the wrist, and be floor-length, opening in front. To maintain the conservative image, I had harem pants designed for wearing underneath the gown and a full-cut bikini top. It was a gown filled with promise without ever violating good taste.

"The designer and the seamstresses finished the measurements and the sketches, then promised to return in twenty-four hours. I knew enough about sewing to realize that they would have to work around the clock. I also knew that the same gown, purchased in the United States, would cost a minimum of five thousand dollars. Since it was being custom designed, there was no way anyone else could wear it. As I said, it was an impressive display of wealth.

"My hair was long and worn down, held back from my face by a crownlike garland of baby's breath and yellow flowers. It was much like a wedding spray and had been created to coordinate with the gown.

"It was sunset on Saturday night when the Mercedes limousine pulled up to the hotel. I was taken to the Sporting Club which had a massive private dining room walled in by glass on three sides to provide a view of the bay of Monte Carlo. There was one large table in the center of the room, where Riza and I were positioned so that we would have the best view of a large stage that had been erected for the entertainment. On it was an orchestra and a continuing array of acts. As the night progressed, there were production numbers featuring seminude women in the same manner as in the nightclubs in Las Vegas. There were comedians, dancers, and other entertainers.

"The table was equally elaborate. The cloth was burgundy, the China white with a burgundy rim. Instead of centerpieces, a single lilac rose was placed at each setting. Each person also had three glasses, four forks, four spoons, and several knives. It was the most formal array of silverware I had ever encountered and I was bewildered by the arrangement. All I knew was that you start with the silverware farthest away from the plate and work your way in. Everything else I learned by observing the others.

"The light on the table was provided by elegant candelabra, carefully positioned to assure an evenness of illumination. Spotlights adorned the stage.

"The other women were as lavishly dressed as I, though their gowns were older and the styles more old-fashioned. However, they were adorned with custom-designed jewelry made from large diamonds, rubies, and emeralds. One woman wore a necklace with a platinum setting that had layered diamonds going from her neck to her cleavage. The largest stone, a teardrop diamond of fifty carats, easily worth a half million dollars, I later learned, was at her throat. Then the stones decreased in size to only four and five carats at the cleavage. This was planned not only to draw the eye but also to allow for a thinner strand of platinum, since the weight of the lower diamonds was less. Altogether the necklace was worth several million dollars and it was not the most elaborate I witnessed.

"The bracelets the women wore were extremely wide and designed to match both a woman's earrings and necklace. The stones and some of the patterns were repeated. The woman with the fifty-carat, pear-shaped diamond at her throat had matching but slightly smaller two-inch pear-shaped diamonds on each of several rings.

"The display of opulence was made further impressive by the awareness that most of the jewelry was not new. Rather it had been handed down in families from generation to generation. There wasn't a woman at the table, other than myself, who was wearing less than a million dollars in clothing and jewelry, a fact that again reinforced Riza's apparent importance. In addition, I soon learned that all the guests were titled, from the royal families of numerous European countries.

"The meal itself was extremely elaborate. White fish and a wafer-thin raw meat dish were offered as appetizers. The red wine flowed for those who wished the meat, white wine offered with the fish. Both were of a rare and expensive vintage.

"Then came racks of lamb, artfully swirled potatoes, lightly steamed vegetables, and numerous sauces—curry, hollandaise, béarnaise, a ginger-flavored mint jelly. And in between each dish, a sorbet was provided to cleanse the palate. Lime sorbet followed meat; orange sorbet followed fish.

"Champagne was the beverage of the evening, the bottles turned upside down in an endless array of ice buckets when they were finished. Keeping the bottles on the table and being certain they never ran out was part of the show of opulence Riza used to dazzle me.

"When the desserts came, they were flaming crepe dishes and cherries jubilee. Café au lait, extremely strong by American tastes, was also offered. These were followed by a liqueur, the glass for which was adorned by an artfully cut orange rind that was set on fire. It was both dramatically colorful and a taste I had never before experienced.

"Throughout dinner there were singers, comedians, and, oddly, a shadow maker. He positioned himself in the spotlight so he could make silhouettes of a variety of animals with his hands. It was like watching an act for a children's party and I was surprised to see it, even though he was quite good. The comedians were apparently quite good as well, at least it seemed that way from the laughter that rippled throughout the table. Unfortunately they spoke no English and I had no idea what they were saying.

"Finally Riza asked me to accompany him onto the dance floor in front of the stage. As I did, I looked down and realized that the dance floor was made of a special glass and it was directly over the bay. Discretely positioned underwater lights illuminated the depths. I had never encountered anything quite like it.

" 'Janelle, I want you to take the job in Iran,' said Riza. He was dressed in a tuxedo like the other men. 'I know how much the shah will delight in you. In fact, I'd like to surprise him by having you come to his birthday party.'

"Again I explained how thrilled I was to be offered the job but also how much my career meant to me. I would be giving up everything familiar, everything I felt that I wanted, to move to a new country.

"Still he would not take no for an answer. He smiled again and said, 'I have a little surprise for you.'

"Then, as we stood on the dance floor, I looked through the glass wall at the bay. Suddenly a rocket flew into the air, exploding. Then another one was launched, and another. I was mesmerized by a growing fireworks display, cascading colors lighting the sky.

"For twenty minutes we stood together, entranced by the spectacle he had arranged. And when the grand finale came, dozens of rockets exploded red, white, and blue patterns in honor of my homeland.

"And then the evening was over, Riza making it clear that he wanted my decision in the morning. I had seen the wealth his country could provide. I recognized the power that this man, whoever he was, could muster. I was convinced that the promises of wealth were genuine. I would be a mistress, but my pay would be beyond my greatest dreams.

"Yet somehow I knew it was wrong. I was unaware of the international political situation that would disrupt Iran. I was unknowing of the violence to come. I could not imagine the shah having to flee a nation in turmoil, dying outside his native land while hostile forces took over. All that was still in the future. I only sensed that to agree to Riza's proposal would not be in my best interests.

"My final decision caused Riza to explode with anger. No one had ever refused the shah before, he told me. The shah would be displeased. The shah would be hurt. The shah . . . the shah . . . the shah . . .

"I left immediately, discovering that the generous shah had no intention of paying for my return flight. Money was promised for reimbursement but I never received it.

"It did not matter. I boarded a flight that would eventually return me to Los Angeles. At first I dozed, then did some crocheting, then took one of the news magazines the flight attendants offered me. To my amazement, there was a picture of Riza or, as the caption corrected me, Mohammed Riza Pahlevi, the Shah of Iran."

Janelle did not yield to the shah, but the efforts to which a rich and powerful man went to both please and acquire her were seductive. She craved the excitement, the gifts, the adoration that the kept life-style could bring. For her, like so many others, it was to prove a near fatal addiction.

There is also a second side to being a kept woman. It is a more positive side for the woman who wants companionship, a degree of physical security, and a long-term friendship without the emotional involvement of marriage. Often this woman is older, at least thirty when she enters the life, and frequently has experienced abusive males in her family and/or among men she has dated. She may have been unhappily married or had a long-term live-in relationship with a man who was physically or emotionally abusive. She has come to value her privacy, value extensive time alone. The idea of being kept by a man has tremendous appeal.

"He comes to me for reasons quite different from those he would have if we were married. He does not appear at my condominium when he is under stress and explosive. Such moods, if he has them, are shared with his secretaries, his salespeople, his wife and children. I don't see the dark side of him. I don't know if he has a temper, if he knows how to cut people with his words.

"He comes to me to celebrate our life together, his successful business deals, his personal triumphs. He comes to me when he is hurting and ready to be comforted. He comes to me when he wants to escape what he feels are overwhelming pressures, taking me to the ballet, to a concert, to an expensive dinner, or to a runaway place like Las Vegas or Monte Carlo.

"We're comfortable together because there is nothing to drive us apart. He dresses casually when we have a few days together, but I never see the torn T-shirts, that foul-smelling 'good luck' hat he always wears when fishing with the family in the Bahamas. He told me of a camping trip he took with his wife where he didn't shave or bathe for a week and he only brushed his teeth when he couldn't stand the smell of his own breath. He won't do those things with me.

"We lead a storybook existence. He gets only as close to my emotions as I want him to and he does the same with me.

"Would I marry him? Probably. Or maybe I say that because it is not an option and maybe never will be.

"My father was an abusive drunk who beat up my mother every

Saturday night. She loved it. She always said that it took a 'real man' to stand up to her moods and put her in her place. Being hit was foreplay for them, though I vowed I would never lead the same kind of life.

"So what happened to me? They say you're drawn to the familiar, so maybe I subconsciously knew my first husband would be abusive. He didn't do it often, but the second time around you get the message.

"I had a couple of serious relationships after that, though the men were the same way. Sometimes it was physical. Sometimes it was emotional. Either way, if I kept my distance, I was always safe. Nothing ever happened during the early stages of the relationships.

"I guess what I'm doing with Harold is prolonging the courtship phase forever. He's kept me for several years now and everything has always been perfect. We don't share a real life. We both know that. It's like he has the real world with his wife and kids and job. And he has the world we've created together. That's a world of good sex, laughter, good times. There are no problems here. I suppose you could say that we've come to love each other, though I question that. Love requires far more honesty, commitment, and . . . I don't know . . . vulnerability, I guess. Neither of us lets the other see quite enough for the other to cause irrevocable pain.

"Maybe that's what commitment is really all about. The ability to hurt the other person in ways that are totally destructive and without redemption, yet choosing to not cause that pain. It's knowing that you can literally kill the other person with words, yet choosing never to say those words.

"Harold doesn't know those words that will hurt me and I don't know the ones that will hurt him. I could make a guess, a really good guess, I suppose. But I wouldn't be sure. If we loved each other, really loved each other, we'd have that extra power yet never use it.

"I don't want to love anyone that much again. I want to be safe and what we have is safe. It's like the happiness of a good book, a warm fire, and a fine wine on a cold winter's day. I feel good all over when he's around, yet I get along perfectly well when he's not. I don't think we'll ever stop this arrangement, not even if he could no longer be my sole financial support. We've found everything we want in our arrangement and hopefully he'll stay happily married for the rest of his life so we never have to consider anything else."

A similar perspective, though for different reasons, was stated by

Ronna, now thirty. "I was sixteen and a half when this wealthy actor began keeping me. He was going through a mid-life crisis and his wife was emotionally disturbed, frequently beating their son. He told me that putting me in an apartment of my own would make our being together easier than his trying to see me while I lived with a roommate, having essentially run away from an abusive home life.

"So there I was, living in a beautiful old apartment with real parquet floors and a fireplace in the bathroom. The rent was paid. I never saw the landlord. I had a car to drive, nice clothes, and six hundred dollars a week to spend as I pleased. Six hundred dollars a week was a lot of money back then and I never wanted for anything. I never tried to learn what real life was like because I didn't have to. Why should I have bothered with all that?"

The world of the kept woman is a fascinating one that can be both idyllic and a nightmare depending upon the reasons for the relationship. Yet the question remains as to why a woman would want to be kept and why a man would keep her. After all, we are at the close of the twentieth century. The American feminist movement has concerned itself with ensuring that women have the freedom to choose any job or life-style they desire. Being kept implies being out of control of one's own destiny. So who are these women? What has happened in their lives to cause them to seek such an existence? And who are the men who feed what is either their pleasure or their overwhelmingly destructive addiction?

2

Once Upon a Time . . .

Americans believe in fairy tales, magic, and happily ever after. Horatio Alger wrote of the American dream at the turn of the century, creating characters who were poor and downtrodden, but determined to have a better life. They were honest, hardworking, fair to others, and invariably rewarded with high-paying jobs, a loving, supportive spouse, and the respect of their friends and neighbors.

Children who fear the unknown evils that lurk in closets, under beds, and in the shadows of night take comfort from fairy tales where, no matter how helpless the heroine, the handsome prince always comes to her rescue. Sleeping Beauty may have been "zapped" by the evil witch for one hundred years, but when the handsome prince leaned over her for a kiss, she was transformed back to the woman she had always been. There was no body odor from a century without bathing, no foul breath from not having brushed her teeth, not even a reduction in her voluptuous figure from her ten decades of fasting. She met her destiny and lived happily ever after.

Early television capitalized on these beliefs. Remember Warren Hull and shows such as "Strike It Rich" and "Queen for a Day"? Women went on the air to tell how hard life had been, to win prizes and have the magic intervention of the "Heart Line," where strangers would call in to assure the contestants of food, clothing, a paid utility bill, or some other need.

The Millionaire told of people who were suddenly given checks for a million dollars, tax-free, to do with as they wished. In more recent times, King Features Syndicate provides newspapers throughout the United States with a column called "Thanks a Million!" in which Minneapolis millionaire Percy Ross gives away money to people whose stories intrigue him enough to respond.

Perhaps we no longer believe in the magic of Aladdin's lamp which held a genie ready to grant three wishes to anyone who rubbed the sides. But we do believe in Las Vegas, Atlantic City, and the "system" that will beat the slot machines, the roulette wheels, the crap tables, or the blackjack dealers.

Those of us who are/have been kept women and the men who keep us take our belief in fairy tales one step further than the rest of society does. We act out our fantasies in real life and we often do it on a global scale. The only problem we encounter is that while it is easy to go from "once upon a time" to the moment when the handsome prince sweeps us off our feet, almost none of us has the maturity to learn how to experience "happily ever after."

We never admit this fact, of course. When one is hurting and scared, as so many of us are during the period when we seek a kept relationship, life is a perpetual lie. To whom would I admit that what I was really searching for was a good father who showed me love by buying me presents? How could I say that I was in psychological conflict with my mother and sisters, women to whom I had not had the courage to reach out, to try to understand, to explain myself and my insecurities? I was trapped in a shell I thought was safe because it seemed to keep the pain of life from entering my created world. Yet the truth is that the protective shell with which we kept women so frequently surround ourselves actually is a way of perpetuating the pain that is trapped inside, slowly eating away at the very essence of what makes us unique individuals.

Fairy-tale Brides

Kept women play a variety of roles in their fantasies, but most of them, if they admitted the truth about themselves, would be Cinderella. Fatherless or without a dominant male figure in childhood, often outcasts in school or loners by choice, they are unappreciated by siblings and others in their immediate spheres. Some think that they are unattractive. Others feel that their looks are unnoticed by a self-centered world. Whatever the case, the first time they go to the ball, or a glamorous party, they are ripe for the advances of a man who recognizes their potential. Sometimes a Cinderella is swept up that very night, fleeing in his Rolls-Royce instead of having to return home and wait until he pursues her with a glass slipper, or at least flowers or an impressive present, to prove his devotion. Sometimes she returns home unfulfilled and disappointed, only discovering days or weeks later the impression she made when he telephones and asks to see her.

A few break the mold enough to enter modeling, acting, or some other glamorous profession where they are seen by millions, adored by thousands, and pursued by dozens. They come to symbolize glamour most men think is unattainable. They become a prize to attain, and make a man feel like a trophy hunter stalking an exotic species he wants to have and stuff and mount to show off to the world. And while the women may deep down know differently, they come to believe that it is better to hang on a wall to be seen and admired than to walk the streets where they have been lost in the crowd.

In a sense, I was lucky. I was attractive enough to enter the glamour world, to travel internationally as a model and an actress. I was always booked more than a year in advance and would have been financially set for life had I not become addicted to the kept life-style. However, I was an addict and that meant I felt compelled to constantly place myself in situations where I had no money, no shelter, nothing but my looks and personality to trade for a place to live. By the time I realized what I was doing to myself, there was no financial cushion I could use to bail myself out.

The greatest problem with the kept life-style is that neither Cinderella nor the rich, famous, and/or powerful Prince Charming knows what to do after each has won the other. Cinderella is quite content with the servants, the clothing, the gifts, and the constant adoration. Yet once she is kept, she knows she is no longer a challenge for the Prince. You don't stalk what you have already caged. Even worse, there are younger, prettier, and/or more pliable women still on the loose. Unless she finds a way to keep the Prince happy—and some Cinderellas practice every type of sex they can learn, go religiously to health spas to maintain their figures, and anoint their bodies and faces with every cream that even hints at stopping aging—Cinderella knows she must campaign for her next Prince. Ideally she will let herself be "lured" away before she can be thrown away. At the least, she wants to have a man she can call when her Prince trades her in for a new model. Ideally she will let herself be kept by a string of men, moving from one to the next, often within the same social circle, until there is no one left and "happily ever after" is but a faded dream.

Prince Charming has a different problem. The point of winning Cinderella is acquiring the most beautiful, most desired woman in all the land. But once he wins her hand, his fellow princes accept the fact that she is no longer available to them. Some see her as an even greater potential conquest, to be wooed and won from their friend Charming. Others forget she exists, becoming uninterested at the sight of her on the Prince's arm. They focus on another young woman who is the most beautiful and desirable, competing with one another for her hand. They even ridicule Charming because he cannot have her, making her more of a challenge and a greater incentive for Charming's ridding himself of his incumbent Cinderella.

The result is that a kept relationship's permanence is measured in weeks, months, or, only on rare occasions, years. Yet the players think that they are winners. How many men can walk with Cinderella on their arm? How many women can be wined, dined, feted, and bedded by Prince Charming? Each is the ultimate conquerer. Yet, as will become obvious in the chapters ahead, each is also the ultimate loser. Cinderella doesn't last forever. She can be kicked back into the ash bin when she is twenty, thirty, forty, or, if she is lucky, fifty. Prince Charming can play the game longer, his money buying him, as he ages, the adoration of the young. Yet even he realizes that that adoration is based more on his power, prestige, and ability to keep a woman handsomely than on his looks, sexual prowess, or rapier wit.

Cinderella sells love. Prince Charming is the buyer. And "happily ever after" is the ultimate fairy tale.

Yet despite all the negatives, the glamour is undeniable. Many women and men fantasize about going to the ball. Most of us like the idea of being viewed as an object of worship, respect, and adoration by the opposite sex. We like the idea of being pampered and desired by the rich, the powerful, the famous. We want to know what it is to dine in restaurants whose prices we could never afford, to be in country clubs our backgrounds would never allow us to join, to stay in suites of luxury hotels we would otherwise never set foot in. Man or woman, in some ways we all want to be Cinderella.

Kept women say that the trappings of the man are important when they are trying to live out a fairy tale. Most women we interviewed were born into poverty or a life-style where hard work by both parents never resulted in their getting very far ahead. A tract house, a good, secondhand car, the ability to pay for bowling and a beer once a week, these were the high points of many of their parents' productive earning years. A few women came from money, private schools, and graduation trips to Europe. The former were seduced by a world they had never experienced. The latter were terrified of losing a life-style they never wanted to leave. Both needed Prince Charming to enter their lives.

There is one other common thread in the lives of the majority of kept women. They have a desperate need for attention from a father figure. Sometimes a father is missing from the home through death, divorce, or abandonment. Sometimes a father is missing emotionally, so involved with his work that he has no time for his daughter. Whatever the case, almost all kept women desperately want male approval. And always that approval is perceived in the form of the man giving them gifts, taking them on trips, giving them houses in which to stay, cars to drive, and/or money to spend. Being in the presence of the rich, the powerful, or the famous makes them feel that they have achieved the approval they desperately need. They have no sense of their own worth except as the man provides it for them, a fact that results in their emotional destruction when younger, more attractive women replace them in the world they dominated for so many months or years.

The Real Prince Charmings

Prince Charmings come in all kinds of packages. Some are young; others old. They may be short or tall, their bodies lean, muscular, fat, or dumpy. They can be nattily attired or dressed in faded denims, T-shirts, and tennis shoes that have seen better days. Some have vast sums of money. Others have political power. Still others are famous. Whatever the case, each dominates a segment of society, is often profiled in the media, and has the image of being strong, sophisticated, desirable, a person whose very presence can make things happen that might be impossible for lesser mortals. Yet each of these men is weak, angry, hurting. Each is carrying his own demons, which is why he is drawn to Cinderella and the other fairy-tale heroines who are kept women.

For example, there is the Politician, a man whose influence crosses over party allegiances because his inherited wealth includes investments in corporations with special interests in oil, banking, and other essential business. He is a power broker, charismatic, and constantly in the news. Yet he is also a womanizer and substance abuser, and he harbors great anger toward women.

The Politician has two types of women—those he keeps and, as he likes to comment to his friends, those who are his "fucks." The latter are campaign groupies, attractive women accepting menial jobs in order to bask in their employer's greatness. Or they are workers who confuse the man with his speeches, seeing him as something more than mortal. Whatever the case, they provide a brief sexual respite from his work, the liaisons occurring in his private office, hotel rooms, or one of his houses.

The ones who are kept receive a greater commitment and get a glimpse of the reality of the man. They stay in an apartment or a hotel suite. They are given a car, clothing, and spending money. Theirs is the hint that a more lasting relationship is possible, though they are eased out of his life within a matter of weeks.

"It seemed like a dream come true," said Miriam. "He flew me first-class to Washington, then put me up in an expensive hotel. I could go shopping, eat anywhere, have the most expensive meal on the menu brought to my room. And always I knew that the man I was seeing on the news and in the magazines was thinking about me, rushing to return to me when he could break away from his work on Capitol Hill.

"At first things were okay. He had no sense of foreplay, just in and out and back to work, but I blamed that on his work load. Even the least dedicated people in Congress seem to work incredibly long hours. I figured he didn't have time for gentle lovemaking and I was so excited about his interest in me that I was ready for him the moment he opened the door. Things just weren't very satisfying physically, but I figured they weren't for him, either.

"Then we got lucky. He had a couple of days when there were no meetings, no public appearances, no reason to travel back to his home state. We had all the time we needed to relax, make love, and share what I thought would be an extremely sensual experience.

"The first time we had sex it was the same thing. In fact, before I got out of the bathroom afterward, he was sitting in the living room of the suite, wearing a robe, reading some position papers for a hearing that was coming up the following week.

"I was annoyed. We had all the time in the world and there he was with his wham-bam-thank-you-ma'am approach. I made some crack, half-joking and half-serious. And that was when I saw a very different side of him."

The politician slapped Miriam's face. "I was shocked and started to leave. But for some reason I decided that he had been under too much stress. I figured he was tired, pressured. He couldn't have meant it.

"I waited a while, leaving him alone while I watched television. Then I went over to him and began rubbing his back, trying to get him in the mood. He reached up and took my hair, pulling my head down as he opened the sash of his robe. He wanted me to work on him orally, something I was uncomfortable doing.

" 'Let's go back to bed,' I said, but he wouldn't hear of it. He said that I wanted it that way, that I knew I did, and that I shouldn't argue or he'd have to get rough again. He was smiling at me, his hand tightening on my hair so it was beginning to feel like he was pulling it out of my head. I was being hurt and it scared me.

"I did what he wanted, stopping before he could do anything, then trying to get him back in the bed. 'We have so much time. Let's make it last,' I told him. And then he just exploded. He asked me if I didn't think he was good enough for me. He told me that hundreds of girls would kill to be where I was, to have him any way he wanted to do it to them. He called me an 'ungrateful bitch' and worse. Then he hit me again. And that's when I realized he liked it. Hitting me was getting him aroused."

Miriam said that what happened next might as well have been rape. She had no interest in continuing any further with the politician, especially when it came to having sex. All she wanted to do was go home and forget she had been so foolish as to yield to her lust for him. But he refused, forcing her onto the bed, entering her when she wasn't ready, then bragging that he had had the best sex of their relationship when he was finished.

"That ended that relationship. I had the feeling that if the bastard hadn't already paid for a round-trip plane flight, I would have had to find my own way back."

The Arab Entertainer was a man who was concerned about his image, not commitment. He made millions of dollars in immensely popular European and American films playing a suave, sophisticated lover. He was an avid card player, expert enough to seldom lose in either tournaments or casinos. He wanted to be able to have a house filled with fine antiques, good food, and a beautiful sex partner wherever he traveled. He believed that such relationships were good for his image and ensured his excellent health. He said that he liked the familiarity of knowing the beautiful women who awaited him as he traveled from country to country, and the variety of being assured that each would be different in the ways she would try to please him.

"I met him in France. He wanted to set me up in a house with servants and an allowance. He was working all over the world and would drop by whenever he could. I would want for nothing but could not see any other men. He just wanted to show me off when he was in the neighborhood. Apparently he had several other women who had agreed to this arrangement. He was quite surprised when I said no."

The Swiss Industrialist: "I met him while working on a documentary in Switzerland. I was doing some of the writing and assisting the film crew in exchange for living expenses, travel, and all the skiing I wanted.

"Jacques was a citizen of the world. I never did learn how many businesses he owned, but he was extremely wealthy.

"He was a man in his late forties or early fifties, balding, overweight, and yet with a style about him. He always looked impeccable in whatever he wore and he seemed to command respect. You noticed him when he entered a room, instinctively knowing that he was important.

"His wife was a beautiful woman of forty and he had an equally beautiful secretary who obviously adored him. They all seemed to have some sort of arrangement, though that was not obvious at the time we met.

"Jacques took me to dinner and questioned me about the documentary. He was genuinely interested in the business-aspects side of film-making and his questions were surprisingly sophisticated. He looked me in the eyes when we talked and he seemed pleased that I was intelligent.

"I had had a number of relationships with guys my age, but they all seemed intimidated by my intelligence. They wanted me to give up my career and take care of them. When they found out I was financially independent, it scared them even more.

"Jacques didn't care about any of that. He enjoyed my mind. He had so much money, the fact that I had a private source of income meant nothing to him. He could not be jealous of me.

"Jacques asked me to stay in Switzerland. He arranged for a place for me to live and took me skiing, to the opera, to expensive restaurants. He had me accompany him to business meetings, encouraging me to participate, something I had never experienced before. He did not try to seduce me, but when we finally had sex two or three weeks into the relationship, it was the most wonderful sex I had ever experienced with a man.

"There's something about older men that's wonderful. The men my age think that great sex is seeing how many times they can come in an hour. A man of forty has the attitude of 'let's see if we can make it last for three hours.' He wants you to experience the slow sensuality of lovemaking. He wants you to be completely satisfied. It's a very different attitude and I had never known anything so wonderful. It was addicting.

"What I never saw was how subtly he was manipulating me. He wanted me to have a career. He encouraged me when we talked about the documentary work I was doing. He was genuinely interested in what I had to say. Yet the documentary crew finished its work and moved on without me. I had no connections with Swiss companies. I was respected. I was enjoying the greatest lovemaking I had ever experienced. I thought I had achieved complete happiness, yet I had actually given up everything for this man.

"It was several months before I realized what was happening. Jacques gave me the use of his Rolls-Royce. I got to know his wife and the three of us often went out together. He never said that I was being kept by him, yet I can't see how she didn't realize that something was happening. I had absolutely no worries, plenty of physical pleasure, and none of what I had been working for in my career.

"Then he began bringing up ideas he wanted to try. He wondered if I would be interested in having his secretary join us for sex. He did not push the matter. He did not threaten to stop keeping me. It was an idea to be accepted or rejected, and nothing changed when I told him no."

But the situation did change. Elaine, the woman involved, began thinking about what was happening. She realized that there was no commitment on the part of the industrialist. No matter how a ménage à trois is conducted, the intensity of the sex act that is possible between one man and one woman is eliminated. With three in bed, the situation suddenly becomes impersonal. The man might be a voyeur. The man might simply want to heighten physical sensations prior to orgasm. But he does not want to experience the intensity that can arise when one man and one woman work together to ensure each other's happiness in bed.

Then she realized that something else had been happening to her during this time. She had willingly abandoned everything in which she believed in order to stay with Jacques. He might or might not have been in love with her, though he certainly had no intention of leaving his wife, a fact he made quite clear from the start. She was a pleasurable convenience, a woman he seemingly respected yet one he controlled regardless. She had become a submissive, malleable plaything who had altered her life for his approval. Maybe that was what Jacques had desired from the start. Maybe Jacques had no idea she would act in such a manner. Whatever the case, the reality in which she was living was intolerable. She had to leave.

"What I can't help but wonder is whether or not I would do it again. If the man was single. If I felt he respected me. If my money and my intelligence weren't stumbling blocks. If . . . If so many things. Do I dislike myself so much that I would marry a man who would want me in a position where I could not do what I want to do?

"It had been so subtle with Jacques. Subtle, yet obvious, I suppose, if I ever bothered to look. I just didn't want to bother, I guess. Or maybe I was afraid to know that part of myself."

The Billionaire Industrialist: The truth about his background is unknown, his past a series of conflicting stories. Some say he was born in poverty, a street child who went from being a part of a gang of street thieves to heading various successful businesses. Others say he was born into wealth he knew how to use to his own advantage. Whatever the truth, he was a millionaire businessman by the age of twenty-five, his money officially coming from various real estate deals throughout Europe. Later he involved himself in myriad businesses, from perfume factories allegedly used to process smuggled drugs at night, to international arms sales. His weapons usually supplied both sides of a conflict so that, no matter who triumphed, he would be an honored part of the new leadership.

The Billionaire Industrialist sees women as playthings. He wants them to be flawless adornments on his private jets, his helicopter, and/or his oceangoing yacht. They are to be adornments who look good at parties, are intelligent, yet know when to disappear from the conversations taking place. Frequently, when he tires of them, he will request that they act as an escort for one of his male guests. There is the unspoken suggestion that it is all right if the woman spends the night with the guest, his way of saying he is no longer interested.

"He uses a madam in Beverly Hills to screen his women for him. She doesn't send him prostitutes. She finds actresses, models, debutants . . . young women of beauty and intelligence who seem to be looking for a little excitement. Then she arranges to introduce them to him at a party that seems quite innocent. If he likes them, he will take them with him to his apartment in New York or his place in Rome, or London, or one of the Arab countries where he operates. They will want for nothing so long as he is interested in them, and the madam is paid a ten-thousand-dollar finder's fee for each girl.

"There is nothing serious about the relationships and many are not very long-term. He uses the madam the way some people use a singles bar. And with his money, the ten thousand dollars he pays for each girl he sees later is no different from the cost of a few beers the average man is going to buy while trying to pick up someone he's interested in."

The Jewelry Magnate: "We met at a party in Beverly Hills," said Sheila. "He lives in Manhattan and has a fabulous business. He was quite worldly and knows everyone in show business because he has the kind of quality merchandise people buy for show and for investment. He told me that he comes out here for varying amounts of time and he finds it delightful to have a beautiful woman to escort.

"I laughed and told him that if he wanted to take me to expensive restaurants and treat me to fine wines, I'd be happy to let him. He laughed, too, but he asked me out for the next evening and we went to this little French restaurant I had never known existed. There were no menus and the waiter told us what they had to eat. He had me order anything I wanted, then bought me Dom Perignon. It wasn't the first time I'd been out like that, but it was the first time that the man was so comfortable with what he was doing. The meal, the drinks, even the prices were so familiar to him, it was like watching someone else eat at McDonald's.

"He was a perfect gentleman all evening. I was the one who suggested he spend the night at my place because I felt I owed him something for the evening. It wasn't much of a reason, yet I really enjoyed the sex and realized that I did like the man.

"We spent the next two nights together, then he flew back to New York. I didn't think anything more about it until he came back to Beverly Hills six weeks later. That was when he made me the proposition. He would pay for an apartment for me, give me a spending allowance, give me the use of a credit card, and lease me a car if I would agree to be available anytime he flew out.

"The only thing I had to do was be available to him when he called. He didn't care what I did when he was in New York so long as I was exclusively his when he came to Beverly Hills. However, I did have to be discreet about anything I did, the apartment being his exclusive territory even though it would be under my name.

"I liked the idea and I liked things even more when I met this guy who lived in Malibu. He wasn't much for brains but he was great in bed. I didn't tell him about my arrangement but I also never let him stay overnight at my place and he knew not to call me. I checked in with him when I wanted him and that was okay.

"I don't know when I got careless. It was probably about two years into the relationship. All I know is that I decided to let the guy from Malibu stay overnight with me. He brought some clothing which he left in my place, both of us figuring it would be no problem. Anyway, there came a time when the jeweler came in from New York without calling. It was a rush flight and he couldn't let me know until he was at the airport. Everything was so rushed that I forgot to get rid of my boyfriend's clothing and shaving supplies. The jeweler found them and cut me off.

"It was so strange. He knew I was not going to be sitting on my rear end, waiting eagerly for his return. He didn't seem to care that I might be having an affair sometime. He just didn't want anything happening in the apartment where he kept me, and when I broke that rule . . . It was just a good thing I saved some of the spending money he allowed me or I would have been in trouble."

Examples of Prince Charmings can go on and on. They come from all walks of life, sharing only the fact that they have power, influence, wealth, and/or great fame. Some want sex. Others want conversation. Others want a decoration for when they are in public. Still others want a play toy with whom they can indulge their most vicious fantasies. Yet no matter how they appear, no matter what their personalities, the kept women will do anything to gain their approval.

3

The Two Sides of the Kept Woman

"I was thirty-three years old when I got involved with Hal. I had a good job, my own apartment, plenty of friends, and the ability to do anything I wanted. Even my mother had stopped talking with me about marriage, accepting the fact that she was not going to be a grandmother because I was having too much fun to want to bother with children.

"I had dated, of course. I had had some serious affairs. But I never wanted to be totally involved with someone.

"Do you know what it's like to live alone? When I come home from work and I want to relax, I can take off my blouse, take off my bra and toss it in the corner, and put on an old T-shirt. I'm basically a slob who keeps the essentials clean but if things stack up for a couple of days, I don't care.

"Now Hal comes in with me after we've been out on the town, I toss my clothes where I always do, and he thinks I'm wild, uninhibited. He tells me that his wife's too formal. He says she can't be spontaneous with her lovemaking like me. I'm a slob, but he thinks I'm being sexy.

"Let's say I was with him more than the two or three days a week we're together. The fantasy would be gone. He wouldn't see me as being uninhibited. He'd see me for the slob that I am.

"You don't know Hal, but I can tell you what he'd say. 'Jesus Christ, Jessica. You're a pig. Put your clothing away when you take it off. What will people think if they see us living this way?' That's what he'd say. A woman who's being kept isn't hassled the way a wife is."

Dr. John Kappas, a psychologist in Van Nuys, California, who has worked extensively with kept women over the years, explained another aspect of the kept-woman situation. "It prolongs the honeymoon stage of the relationship for the whole time they are together," he said. There is a heightened excitement that married couples usually lose after from one to three years of marriage.

Dr. Kappas also described the typical kept-woman relationship he has found when both parties are fully aware and accepting of the relationship in which they are living. The man will usually be rather quiet, withdrawn, with work being his primary interest. He is the type who will attend a party or a board meeting, sitting away from the action, watching everything but unable to feel comfortable participating. He is married, but he probably married for the wrong reasons. He may have been excited by the woman's looks or the way she responded to his attention. They may have enjoyed sex together, his experiencing more desire than he had with women in the past. Whatever the case, he probably did not truly get to know her, becoming comfortable with the relationship without developing it to such a level that he truly knew how she thought, her plans for life, and other factors needed to sustain them. As a result, she became a good wife and mother but he became bored with her. They did not share the work that was the primary focus of his life.

This type of man will be drawn to a woman with whom he works. She will usually be his opposite, outgoing where he is shy, comfortable working crowds at parties or talking freely during business conferences. She may be in sales and quite good at what she does.

There are several reasons for the attraction. One is the fact that the woman works with him on a regular basis. Since work is a primary focus of his life, being able to talk with someone who fully understands what he does is important to him. If his wife were to work in the office with him, he would probably never consider an affair. But because she does not share the business side of his life, something that is extremely important to him, he feels drawn to a woman who does share this aspect of his life.

The woman will probably work under the man, whether in a department reporting to him or more personally, for example, as his secretary. "She feels so compatible, so comfortable with this particular person, that he finally talks her into an affair. And then what happens is she leaves her job and divorces her husband and continues this affair, but it doesn't turn to marriage. And eventually what happens is she becomes the kept woman and years pass by. The longer it goes, the more years pass by, the more urgent she becomes to hang on to this relationship." Whatever the case, she continues to look up to him and respect him.

Finally, the man will be totally honest with her. There are no false promises about leaving his wife. He will make it quite clear to her that such a situation will not happen. This may be because there are children or, more likely, because his financial picture is such that he cannot afford both a divorce and to continue in his present work. A settlement may be so necessarily great that he would have to sell critical aspects of his assets or use cash he needs to continue functioning the way he has been. But the important point is that he is honest. He does not make promises he has no intention of keeping. The woman knows what she is getting into and can accept or reject him on that basis.

Both the man and the woman commit within these parameters. Frequently they are monogamous (except for that little matter of his wife), staying together for twenty years or longer.

Dr. Kappas mentioned one of the more unusual such long-term commitments, unusual in the sense that the man made his commitment not once but several times, honoring them all. "One man, whose wife was a patient of mine, had a business but no one really knew where he made his money, not even his wife. He had a beautiful house, the children were healthy, they attended the best schools, and he would come and go as he pleased. She could never question him about his work, yet she never lacked for anything.

"One day the man had a heart attack. He was taken to the Cedars of Lebanon Hospital where the staff went through his wallet and found a pile of six different first names all with the same last name. They didn't know which were daughters and which was the wife, so a nurse got on the phone and called all of them. None were in, but all had answering machines. She left a message on the machines of all of them.

"About three hours later, all six women showed up at the hospital. They began looking at one another. They were all his mistresses who had taken his last name at his request, though he never married them. The only one who was his real wife was the one he had had kids with. They each knew about the wife but not about one another. And they were all about the same age, some of them having been kept by him for at least twenty-five years in different parts of California. They had come to the hospital from Anaheim, Santa Ana, Beverly Hills, Truesdale, Van Nuys . . . He had them scattered.

"They all had homes. They all had regular lives. He had supported them, saying, 'I'm a businessman. Don't ever question me. So long as I take care of you, that's all that matters.'

"They all had taken his last name because he didn't want them to be embarrassed by their neighbors. And they all had changed their names legally to his. That was the way they wanted it. And they all showed up.

"This guy's not dead. He's had a serious heart attack. He's lying in bed and he looks up and sees the five of them and his wife. And he turns green, though there's a little smile on his face.

"His wife said that when he smiled, they looked at one another and they all laughed. Then he just closed his eyes and looked asleep.

"They all gave him up but they all became best friends. His wife said that they still talk about him. She tells her family about it. And he still supports them. He's quite old and doesn't run around as much. But he still takes care of them even though they left him."

Oddly, in these positive relationships, keeping a woman does not always mean the man has large sums of money. Dr. Kappas mentioned one man who earned from twenty-five thousand to fifty thousand dollars a year, the higher figure only in recent times. While this represented a higher-than-average standard of living, the figure was not large enough to keep women in the manner which our fantasies imagine. Instead, he kept a waitress he found attractive. She continued to work but he supplemented her take-home pay by approximately two hundred dollars per month. They also went out together from time to time, though those were the only costs.

Many of the kept women in positive relationships did not experience the trauma so many mistresses discuss. They were not left alone on holidays, weekends, or birthdays. The men had long-established patterns of being workaholics who were comfortable only if they went to the office for some portion of each day, seven days a week. For example, their wives were accustomed to their being with the family Christmas morning, opening presents, going to church, eating an early meal, and acting like any other doting husbands and parents. However, then, instead of curling up in front of the television set while the children played with their new toys, they would go to the "office." In reality, they were spending time with the women they kept, though their families never questioned.

Similar situations often occurred on weekends. The office work routine was so familiar, the family planned around it. These men would not be called at the office. They simply would not be reachable and the rest of the family would engage in whatever activities they desired.

While there is a positive side to the kept-woman experience, at least for some of the women who are being kept, the negative side is often the most fascinating and the most tragic. This is the case with the woman who is insecure with relationships, who has been seduced by the life-style, and who is constantly trying to reclaim the role of Cinderella at the ball.

What motivates the woman is frequently trauma from her childhood, a period of her life when she often experienced the horrors of the damned. One kept woman, who worked in high positions in banking when she was not being kept, while a teenager had been sexually abused by her father. He was a minister in a respected evangelical church and considered one of the most revered men in the community. Her mother constantly told her that she must obey her father, who, in her mother's eyes, could do no wrong. The woman felt that there was no one to tell who would listen; no one who might believe her. She had to endure the abuse, determined that when she grew up, no man would ever dominate her. She would always be in control. She would always have men paying for the privilege of being in her presence.

When Ted and I first began researching this book, I was afraid to tell the story of my own childhood. I suffered from what many addicts call "terminal uniqueness." I thought I was unusual, that no one had endured what I had experienced. Yet once others were interviewed I realized that the pain I felt was experienced by many, the pressures that molded me very similar to what many kept women had known.

As a model, I earned a six-figure income for many years, yet, as I have mentioned, I was determined that I would always have to be rescued and kept by the wealthy, powerful men in my life. I gave away everything to ensure my own helplessness, at the same time pretending that I had power because they continued to desire me.

Leslie McRay's Story

I was once considered one of the most beautiful women in the world. I was under contract as the representative of a major cosmetics company. I represented the department of tourism for a foreign country eager to lure American tourists. My face adorned the covers of magazines throughout the world. My anatomy was so perfect that my hips alone were under contract to one of the largest, most sophisticated women's magazines in the nation. My income was several hundred thousand dollars at a time when a family of four could be comfortable with an income of ten thousand dollars per year. I have been successful in advertising sales, produced television pilots, had a talk show, and otherwise achieved more in slightly over forty years than most people achieve in a lifetime. In theory I should be financially independent, emotionally secure, maintaining a healthy self-respect.

Instead, I have been a deeply troubled woman at times, currently living from paycheck to paycheck from a job I do not enjoy. My weight fluctuates according to my self-image. My walls are adorned with photographs taken during my days as a world-class model. My VCR holds tapes of past films I have made. And my emotions are torn by my periodic inability to respect myself for who I am, not what I think others want me to be. I am an addict to a life-style to which I know I dare not return, a life-style that caused me to temporarily sell my soul in order to live out a hopelessly distorted fairy tale.

I came from a background of poverty and hard times, which is one thread among many kept women. My achievements should have given me a sense of my own drive and inner strength. Instead, I spent or gave away everything I ever earned in order to be perpetually helpless, a little girl who needed a "father" to buy me presents in order to survive. While my own family history is as unique to me as the histories of many women we interviewed for this book are to them, my emotional responses were typical of almost all the others. I was lucky, though. I am one of the few kept women to understand how the past molded the time I spent in the arms of the White House adviser, the extraordinarily wealthy Philippine businessman, the record industry executive, and all the others. I have also seen the destructive end that can occur when a woman does not get control of the addiction, eventually spending the night in my car, "camped" in the parking lot of a Beverly Hills shopping mall, waiting for a Prince Charming to whom, at forty, I had become an overaged "joke."

I was born in a small Western town of a thousand people, where the economic situation consisted of only two options—times were either hard or harder. Standard Oil had drilled a number of wells which were going dry and were abandoned soon after my birth. There were also a few ranches, most of the men in the community working for the owners rather than owning any of the land themselves. The men usually went to work as teenagers, serving as roustabouts in the oil fields and laborers on the ranches. They worked until their bodies could take no more abuse, becoming old men by the time they were thirty if they lacked the skills or the money to flee to a larger city with greater opportunity. Sex and alcohol were the main sources of recreation, so the town was rife with large families, rampant alcoholism, child and spouse abuse. Drunken revels, battered wives, and scarred children were so normal, a happy home life might have been investigated by county welfare to learn why the people were different.

My mother at fourteen years old was so beautiful that despite her tender years she looked like the movie actress Donna Reed. She was also the oldest of six children, none of whom had enough to eat. When she informed her mother that she wanted to marry her boyfriend, a "man" of seventeen who looked like a double for Clark Gable and had the muscular body that comes from making a living breaking wild horses and working in the oil fields, her mother was delighted. Her daughter would eat better from the meager wages of her son-in-law than she ever could at home.

I was born when my mother turned fifteen, and two sisters were added within the next two years. I never understood the courage my mother would show during the next few years, the strength and maturity despite her age. She was what many social workers call a "baby having babies," and the results were stressful beyond her years. The situation was destructive at best, yet the teenage marriage saved her own family from gnawing hunger because it reduced the number of people at home who had to survive on my grandparents' scanty earnings.

If my mother had been able to stay home with us kids, life might have been a little easier. But good wages for a teenage boy like my father were not good wages for a family. Mother had to go to work and a baby-sitter had to be hired. Unfortunately this meant paying as little as possible so the cost would not come too near to matching my mother's meager earnings. And this left us children open to potential abuse, a fact that would have horrified my mother had she been able to anticipate such a possibility.

The sitter told me it was a game. She would lick me between my legs and I was supposed to do it to her. I didn't like it and knew instinctively that it was wrong. She didn't threaten me or anything during what I know now was oral sex. She called it only a game and I just decided I didn't want to play that game. I never told anybody because I never realized I was being molested.

I later learned that my experience was the most difficult form of molestation a child can experience. There is no sense that a serious problem has occurred, and when you grow older, you worry that because you were not hurt in the way so many victims are, you must have done something to cause it. The incidents become dirty little secrets that gnaw away at your subconscious mind, making you feel guilty instead of the victim you really are. But those feelings also ensure that you are not likely to tell, letting the emotions fester well into adulthood, living with pain that could have been ended had you just known to tell what happened.

There were other tensions in my family. My father had mixed feelings for us. He was the first generation in his European family to be born in the United States and he looked upon his firstborn child as being special. He seemed to take great pride in me and liked showing me off to his friends. Unfortunately this was taking place during a period when he was becoming increasingly estranged from my mother.

In his mind, my father was a happy-go-lucky man who liked to work hard and drink hard. He liked to go to an area bar after work, drinking with his friends and, frequently, with his mother. I know now that he was an alcoholic, even at that early age, using his paycheck for liquor rather than his constantly growing family.

The pregnancies caused my parents to quickly grow apart from each other. At first they managed to play house, obtaining a small white house with a picket fence on land so harsh that weeds had to fight for survival. It was a luxury few people in town could afford, success more frequently meaning the purchase of a trailer home on a tiny plot of land side by side with your neighbors. My grandfather owned his own shoe repair shop and that made him one of the most ¬uccessful men in town. One of my uncles went into the junk and scrap-metal business and that also made him successful by local standards.

Pregnancies, hard work, little money, endless drudgery, and a husband who was frequently drunk were not what my mother expected from life. She also resented the attention that I was receiving while my two sisters were ignored.

My father used to take me to the bar with him, setting me on the counter where I would sing and dance. He played the harmonica professionally in a country band. It was the type with the stand and the amplifier—a professional instrument, not the cheap kind you can buy in dime stores. He also played the guitar. It was natural for me to try to be musical in order to please him.

I began spending all my time at home by the radio, singing and dancing to the music so I could earn Father's approval when he came home. When I did well, he rewarded me by taking me to the bars and showing me off to his friends.

The family situation deteriorated rapidly by the time I was five. My father was almost never at home, his mother encouraging him to leave his marriage because his wife and three children were holding him down. My mother was frequently away from the house, trying to earn money to support us, having to make us children spend time with relatives. Then, to add to the problems I was facing, my great-grandfather, a mentally disturbed man, attacked me while I was playing in a basement.

I couldn't have been more than five. I was in the only dress I owned, my family lucky to afford one dress a year for me. There was a house being built that had the basement in and steps leading up to a door but nothing else. I used to play on the steps, feeling the sun that came through the doorway.

One day my great-grandfather, who everyone said was senile, came down in the basement when I was playing. He started his own game, getting down on all fours, then crawling up the staircase toward where I was sitting. I was scared, knowing something wrong was happening but not realizing that I should move. Suddenly he grabbed my dress and tore it, then began sucking on my chest in the area of what were nonexistent kid breasts. I was terrified. I knew he was doing wrong, but I never told anyone afterward. What seems strange now is the fact that no one ever said anything about my torn dress.

That first molestation led to my having a series of nightmares as I slept, dreams that caused me to fear sex for many of my adult years. They were consistent and surprising, considering my age when they started, yet I remember them vividly more than thirty-five years later. In each dream I was tied to a wall while a second wall, directly opposite, pressed against me, penetrating rather than crushing me.

The divorce, when it occurred, was the result of the alcoholism. My father was everyone's friend in the bars. He bought rounds of drinks for the house, spending his paycheck when he should have used it for our family's needs. My mother became disgusted when our family's refrigerator was ordered repossessed for nonpayment.

It took great courage for my mother to file for divorce. She had no money, little education, and job opportunities that were severely limited. She knew that she would not be able to keep the family together, yet she was determined to do her best. The sad part was that I would not understand the hell she was going to experience and I would not understand how I would misperceive her role in all this. I came to resent her through no fault of her own, then became so disturbed myself that, as an adult, I was never able to bring myself to truly discuss what she endured.

At the time, I became a pawn in the divorce, a means for my father to get back at his ex-wife. He enlisted the aid of his brothers, who my mother trusted, to effect his plan.

The brothers would come to the house and take me with them, using whatever excuse my mother would accept. She had to start working two jobs to support the family, so any help in taking care of the children was appreciated. What she did not realize was that the brothers were taking me to meet with my father.

The reality of my father's actions were quite different from how I interpreted them. I became his date, his special child. His wife was forgotten. His other two children were forgotten. I was the center of his world, or so I thought.

First there would be breakfast at the small café next to my grandfather's shoe repair shop. There I would eat chili, cherry pie, and a glass of milk, the same breakfast my father enjoyed. Then we would go to Woolworth's where he would buy me anything I wanted, a not very expensive proposition since a five year old's desires are fairly cheap. However, to me, everything was special. I was being taken to the finest restaurant I had ever seen to dine, and I was being showered with gifts from the fanciest store I could imagine.

He became my total male love source. He asked me if I wouldn't rather be with him than with my mother, and of course I wanted to be. He was treating me like a princess.

He kept telling me I would have to run away. He told me I would have to make myself so unpleasant toward my mother that she would send me away. Then we'd be happy forever.

My father did not want my two sisters because they looked radically different from me. My appearance was that of the dark, sultry European. The other two girls took after our mother's Irish appearance. He said that only I was his, though he knew full well that he was the father of all three girls. My mother would never have cheated on him, though his comments must have hurt her deeply.

I planned my whole life around getting rid of this horrible witch lady who was keeping me from being with my dad. He kept saying that I would have to be really bad. I would have to do terrible things and run away a lot. He said that eventually the police would just give me to him.

When I went home, I would try to be feisty and ornery. But it was totally against my nature. It was silly and it was never going to work.

However, my father created a dream in me; he created a fantasy in me that stayed with me my whole life. He made me want something I could never achieve; I could not have.

There was never an effort to run away, however. I didn't know where to go. I didn't know how to find him. It was just futile. I resented my mother desperately but could do nothing about it.

The toys and gifts I received were meant to cause additional problems for my mother. My father knew that there would be sibling rivalry each time I brought home presents that were not meant to be shared with my sisters. However, my mother also was aware of the potential problem, taking the gifts and hiding them so there would be no difficulties with the other children. The rivalry was avoided, but unable to understand the reasons behind her actions, I came to hate my mother for denying me my father's "love" offering.

I know now how hard that must have been on her. I realize that by my father's actions, he robbed me not only of his love and attention, but also of any possible relationship with my mother. The difficulty we have in talking today stems from those experiences that were actually vicious manipulations of us both. Yet such knowledge is not available to a child. Only immature, often irrational emotions, a fact I suspect that he well knew.

Although no one could have anticipated the problem, I was also becoming extremely disturbed about my sexuality. I blamed myself for the divorce, thinking that it related to what I was certain was my father's desire for me. He loved me. He wanted me. And my mother kept getting in the way.

There was also a sense that other males wanted me, a belief intensified when I was six and experienced yet another molestation. This time the molester was a teenage cousin with whose family we were staying while I was recovering from having my tonsils removed in the hospital. I put on a frilly dress, decided that I looked especially pretty, and was delighted when my cousin asked me to sit on his lap while he read me fairy stories. However, the minute I was settled, his hand wandered, his fingers poking between my legs. The pain was intense and I became quite frightened, yet I was convinced that I must have done something to cause him to take such action.

Despite the guilt feelings, I knew that his actions had been wrong. I told my mother, who became enraged. The boy was punished and I felt more secure than in the past. Yet still nothing was right for me.

My mother began working at Walgreen's, serving malts over the counter. She worked two shifts until she could become a dental assistant, yet even then she was seldom home. We children had to be taken wherever we would be safe.

The next few years were nightmares for me and my sisters. There was a Catholic orphanage that would board children whose parents could not care for them. There were aunts and uncles who would take us in for short periods of time. Yet no matter what the situation, all we knew was that we were always being shuffled from place to place.

My mother felt that it was necessary to try and give our family some stability. This meant a new marriage, something she pursued with great enthusiasm. There were three marriages while we were being raised, and a fourth that took our family to California.

Each marriage meant the same concerns. First there would be no children around, we sisters remaining in the orphanage. Then we would be introduced to the prospective father. We had to be on our best behavior, auditioning for each man as though we were in show business and it was our last time to be a "star." It was a role I instinctively understood, flirting and being the best child I could possibly be.

Each audition was successful, yet the family never stayed together. My mother only knew to meet men in bars, invariably picking individuals who were weak alcoholics. They would stop working and let Mother care for them until they became so abusive, demanding, and/or violent that she got a divorce. Then we children would be returned to the orphanage and the pattern would repeat itself.

I learned that I had to be the best at whatever I did in order to have a chance for any happiness. Ideally I needed to be perfect, a goal impossible to attain. Yet I tried. Whatever I did, I always had to work harder at it, be better at it, than anyone else. Then maybe my mother would love me. Maybe we kids wouldn't have to go back to the orphanage or stay with relatives. Maybe my father would return or take me away forever.

I was desperate for attention and affection. There were no adults with whom I was close. There were few friends because we sisters stayed such a short period of time everywhere we lived. There were no pets, nothing to call my own. The only answer was to turn to the world of my imagination.

Each time we moved into the home of one of my relatives, I hoped for some stability in my life. Unfortunately it never came from the people around me.

For example, there was one aunt and uncle who took in us children but felt that that was where their responsibilities ended. They were cold, neither physically nor verbally demonstrative. When my uncle went to work, my aunt started to clean. She had a fetish about cleanliness and forced everyone in the house to cooperate. There was never praise, just an end to the complaints about the dirt if we did a good job.

I was desperate for someone with whom I could talk. There was a swing set in the backyard that frequently was ignored by the others. Whenever possible, I would go outdoors and pretend that the swing set was my closest friend. I would race outside as soon as my chores were complete, grabbing the metal sides, pressing my face against the swing set as a different child might hug a teddy bear. I talked to it, telling it my secrets, my hopes, and my dreams. I would kiss the cold metal of the bars, gaining comfort in the only thing that was stable in my life.

In another instance, I found a bird's nest that was momentarily abandoned. I took one of the eggs and sneaked it to my bed, being careful to keep it hidden, warm, and safe from being cracked. I held the egg, talking to it, certain that I would be able to hatch a baby bird that I could call my own. It would be a living, breathing being I could nurture and love. But the egg failed to hatch and I eventually sneaked it back outside to the yard.

Most of the time I was forced to be in the orphanage. It was run by Catholic nuns, the building consisting of dormitories and a school.

No matter where I lived, for nine years my thoughts were always about my father's returning to get me. He would find me, take me away, and we would live happily ever after, just the two of us. He would hug me, sing to me, and play with me. Everything would be perfect when he took me away.

The loneliness was intense, yet with it was a desire to please. If I was good enough, my father would return. If I was good enough, there would be no more orphanages, no more strange foster homes. If I was good enough . . .

My mother decided that she was going to live her life through me. I was going to do everything she had wanted to do. Whenever she had us kids at home, I was given baton-twirling lessons, singing lessons, dance lessons . . .

The baton twirling began shortly after the first divorce. I was enrolled in a six weeks' course that was held during the summer when the children were not in school. I was the youngest student in the class, the least coordinated, yet one of the more determined. If this would win my mother's approval and keep me from being farmed out to another family, then I would do my best. Unfortunately, determination does not compensate for the natural lack of coordination so common with children of that age. By the end of the six weeks, my body was covered with bruises from hitting myself with the baton. I was miserable, yet I won a gold medal for my achievements. The fact that I was the only child so young and was thus not competing with anyone else may have accounted for my winning, but I was unaware of that fact. All I knew was that my mother was proud of me and so the pain I had endured was worth it.

What I did not expect was to be informed that I was going to be competing for prizes in the rodeo. My mother enrolled me in a state competition against four other girls, an event that would take place during the most important competition in the area.

For working ranchers in the West, the rodeo is one of the most important events of the year. It is a time when ranch hands compete for prize money in events that relate to their daily work. They wrestle steers, ride wild horses, rope steers, and otherwise engage in difficult, often dangerous competitions. Most of the community turns out to watch, enjoying both the events and a show that is put on as part of the entertainment. The year I first took my six weeks of baton twirling, the show was to consist of a baton-twirling competition and parade. I was to be one of the stars.

The experience was both frightening and dreadful for me. The other girls were older and experienced, having trained as baton twirlers for several years, performing at their schools and competing in many previous events. They all had costumes and knew a variety of acrobatic tricks that enabled them to excel. I had no costume, just a blouse and shorts, and was able only to turn the baton, not toss it in the air or engage in various tricks while it was spinning.

I didn't even have my own music. I had to borrow some other girl's.

The baton twirling was a disaster. I walked onto the field holding my baton because I hadn't learned to walk and twirl it at the same time. Then I did the only thing I had learned. I twirled it around and around my waist. I didn't know how to toss it in the air and catch it like the other girls did. I didn't know how to twirl it from hand to hand in front of me. I just twirled it around and around my waist until the music stopped. I even dropped it once, but I picked it up and kept on twirling. It probably was just two or three minutes, but it was the longest two or three minutes of my life.

In the end, I won a medal. There were five finalists based on age and five medals. As the only competitor in my category there was no way I could lose, though I did not know that fact.

I was sick to my stomach, but I never complained. I just knew that I was going to go out there and do my best. That was what my mother expected of me and we all go out and live up to our expectations.

I know there must have been applause. They always applaud a little kid. I only remember that I was dying inside and afterward I had to march in a parade. It was before the manure was on the grounds and we had to march for miles. It was probably just around the rodeo grounds, but I thought it was miles. I thought it would never end.

When it was over, my mother took me for a chocolate malt. I figured that this was how I would get approval. I had to do what my mother wanted me to do and I had to do it well.

I continued to feel the pressure, the need to be "very good." I began to draw and paint as a creative outlet while still in elementary school. I sold my first watercolor in the sixth grade. I was moving to California and the art teacher was so impressed with my work that she bought what I painted. Ever since then, I've sold every painting I've ever made.

A lot of that skill had to do with the need for my father's approval. When I was with him, I would try to draw what he looked like. He would guide my hand, showing me how to improve. I was around nine then and it was obvious to me that I had to improve my skills to please him. It was another reason to work so hard.

It was at that time, when my fourth stepfather planned to take the family to California, that I had a chance to visit my father. He was remarried and had a new baby, living on acreage large enough for the couple to keep horses, though not actually a working ranch. My mother told me that I was being asked to visit only because my father wanted someone to baby-sit. There was a great deal of truth to her bitter comment, yet I chose to not believe it.

The trip to visit my father was a lonely one, yet I had greater enjoyment than I experienced at home. Most of the time my father was away, working, going to bars to drink, or spending time with his mother. Yet when he was at home, he made certain that I dominated most of his time. This continued to make me feel special, to feel as though there might still come a time when the two of us would always be together.

There were periods when I was aware of the truth, though. I was given the job of mucking out the stalls, an activity I hated. The work was rugged, foul-smelling, and dangerous. An aggressive young colt took a dislike to me and delighted in backing me into a corner of his stall, then tromping on my feet and lightly biting my shoulder. I was frightened and upset, yet when I complained to my father, he just said, "Bite him back."

The second shock of reality came one night when I was supposed to be asleep. I walked down the corridor of the house, going past my father's bedroom, where the door was slightly ajar. He was making love to his wife, a natural act and something he could not anticipate his daughter witnessing.

I watched for a moment at the door, remaining silent, unobserved. My understanding of sex was crude, the knowledge of an abused child, yet I knew that what was happening was pleasurable for my father. I knew that the woman who was with him was giving him something that I could not. I also knew that one day I would use my body the same way. I would seduce my father, whatever that meant, and then I would both control him and keep any other woman from having him.

Leaving my father was extremely difficult. He decided that I should stay with him, and not return to my mother and sisters. However, my mother obtained a court order against him, an order that would send him to jail if I was not returned.

The move to California was an important one. Suddenly there were options that had not existed in the small southwestern towns where I had been raised. My fourth stepfather was a highly successful accountant who was also an alcoholic. When he was sober his earning capacity was great and he would shower his wife with gifts. He bought her expensive clothing, jewelry, and other items, reinforcing in my mind that he must truly love her. I knew from the time when my father took me to Woolworth's that gifts meant love, so their relationship had to be the best possible to imagine. Unfortunately he was also an alcoholic who regularly lost jobs, becoming so destructively violent that the family had to move from city to city.

School was not important to me. I earned extremely high grades when I attended classes because I *had* to earn them. I had to be the best in anything I did, yet the grades were an end in themselves. They were not a means to a better future. They were not a way to assure that I would be able to go to college and prepare myself for a career. All that mattered was love and approval, neither of which I felt I was receiving.

My mother decided that Southern California was where her daughter was going to become a "star." The family lived down the block from Annette Funicello, who had gained fame as being one of the Mouseketeers, the child stars of Walt Disney's Mickey Mouse Club. Studios were nearby, luxury cars roamed the streets, and everybody seemed to have a dream that, with luck and perseverance, could be achieved.

I was enrolled in modeling classes that were meant to train me to win beauty contests. I was still in elementary school, the only girl in my class to be seriously studying makeup, how to walk, and how to dress.

The training was both a delight and a problem for me. The constant moving from city to city had left me hurting and lonely. Each time there was a chance to make friends, the family changed where they lived and we girls had to face another group of strange children in an unfamiliar setting. It would have been easier making the move when I first entered junior high, a time when children are making new friends. But I moved into a school where the children had known each other for at least five years and where there seemed no reason to try and know an outsider. Since I was not only new but was also engaged in extracurricular activities to which the other girls could not relate, I was shunned.

By the time I was a junior in high school, my direction seemed to have become fixed. I was a loner against my will. I had no girl friends, though I did have a boyfriend, the one male whom I trusted with my innermost feelings. Our relationship was intense, the two of us thinking seriously about a future together. Yet my life was changing rapidly and my direction was show business.

It was during one of my dance classes that I was first "discovered." A small theater near the dance studio was putting on a production of *White Cargo*. The female lead had left the show and the director was in need of a fairly tall, good-looking girl with long dark hair, a situation that perfectly fit me. I auditioned, earned the role, and became a "star" two days later. That forty-eight hours of intense activity was all that was left because the play had been ready for production when the lead left the show.

Oddly, I had tremendous stage fright during this period. I had no sense of self-worth, yet discovered that performing seemed to bolster my confidence.

The stage career was met with hostility by my stepfather. School was not so important for me as becoming a star. I began cutting classes in order to take lessons, rehearse, or just hang around the first people who had ever accepted me without question. My grades became terrible and my stepfather wanted me to quit in order to spend more time with my studies.

What I was doing was ten times more important to me than school was. I was trying to make a name for myself. I was trying to create a demand in the world for me.

During this same period, my mother entered me in the Miss Fullerton beauty contest. She felt that her daughter would gain poise and confidence from being a participant. She also arranged for Greg, her hairdresser, to help me with my appearance.

For the first time there was a change in what was taking place in my life. As a beauty contestant, I found people looking at me differently. I had always thought of myself as unattractive, yet Greg tried to kiss me after finishing my hair and seating me under the hair dryer. He was several years older, handsome, and strong. I had no way of knowing that he flirted with all the girls, the younger the better. All I knew was that suddenly I was receiving special attention, attention that both embarrassed and delighted me.

I was uncomfortable on the stage. Walking across a stage in a bathing suit and high heels is not a natural experience. Yet my appearance was what the judges wanted to see and I was crowned Miss Fullerton, the first of more than seventy contests I won. It was also the first major step toward becoming a kept woman.

There was the ribbon, the flowers, the tiara, the microphone shoved near my mouth so I could speak to the audience. All I can remember at that point was thinking, "Oh, so that's what I'm supposed to be. I'm supposed to be a pretty girl!" For the first time in my life I had an identity.

Until that time I had really thought that I was the homeliest girl God had ever put on this planet. I had no identity, no self-esteem.

It was the 1960s, the end of an era for beauty contestants. Marilyn Monroe was still alive and many photographers remembered the story of the photographer who helped discover her. Studios such as Twentieth Century-Fox retained the contract system where beautiful young girls were placed on a salary and trained to be stars. Each contest was a stepping-stone and the winners were given intense attention.

My experience was typical. Photographers approached me to sponsor me in the next contest that was coming along. Each offered to provide information about the contests, assist gaining area businesses to provide the sponsor fee, and help with anything else I needed in exchange for the exclusive right to be the first to photograph me. If I did not win again, they were out a little time. If I became famous, they could fulfill their own fantasies.

That first beauty contest radically changed my life. The contests were still considered legitimate ways to break into modeling and show business careers. Calls came in for modeling jobs. The attention of the press gave me a celebrity status beyond anything I could ever have imagined.

The second beauty contest I entered was the Miss Disabled American Veteran competition, a much bigger event than the name implies. There were five hundred girls seeking the title and the prizes were extremely large. They ranged from a trip through Universal Studios where the winner was to meet Cary Grant to an extensive wardrobe of clothing. There would be swimming with Flipper in Marine Land, a screen test, and even a tiny part in a television show. Not monetary, the value of some of the prizes was publicity that could not otherwise be purchased. Swimming with Flipper, for example, assured photographs appearing in newspapers and magazines throughout the country.

To my surprise and delight, I was the winner. Both my mother and Greg were in the audience, proudly cheering me on. Only my stepfather had failed to show, a fact that reinforced my sense of closeness to my hairdresser and friend.

I was gradually developing a new life-style during this period. School no longer mattered to me, though I remained close to my boyfriend. My mother was extremely supportive, living vicariously through my success. And Greg, the hairdresser, was becoming a close friend and adviser, preparing my appearance before I competed or engaged in any of the activities expected of the winners.

The more successful I became, the more my stepfather became hostile to the family. He began drinking more, apparently because the alcohol lowered his inhibitions enough for him to violently strike out at my mother and us kids. Many was the night that my mother would climb into bed with us girls in an effort to avoid my stepfather's hitting her. He would then come into the room, grab her, and drag her across our terrified bodies. Sometimes I would be able to talk with him, calming him before he became too violent. Other times he was too drunk to hear anything, struck my mother, then stalked off to the other room. It was a nightmare I wanted to flee.

The beauty contests were becoming all-absorbing for me. Some were honest, many rigged, but my appearance fit the image the sponsors wanted to have and so I was almost certain to triumph.

Expensive clothing stores began helping me without charge. The same firm that designed gowns for Marilyn Monroe and Jayne Mansfield, considered the most glamorous actresses of their day, created hand-sewn gowns for me. In exchange they received recognition during the contest, both in programs and in advertising. This assured them that numerous parents whose daughters had yet to be winners would come to them to order gowns. The cost of one gown for me could result in orders from others that would give them substantial profits.

It was during those early, rather heady days of what I saw as my new life that I was offered a ride home by Greg. He had become a close friend and I saw nothing wrong with stopping at his apartment above the beauty shop for a few minutes when he asked me to come with him. However, once inside I realized that he did not want to just be friends. He began kissing me, trying to take off my clothing.

I was five-feet-seven, young, and fairly strong. At first I treated his aggression as a joke. Then I realized that I was fighting for my virginity. He wanted sex with me and was determined to have it.

The struggle became a violent one. I was thrown against the walls, the floor, the furniture. He was more powerful than I was, but he did not want to hit me. He wanted to wrestle me into submission and my resistance added to his arousal. If I ceased struggling, it was obvious that he would rape me. Yet the more I struggled, the greater his physical desire became. Finally, hurt and exhausted, I was pinned to the floor and entered. There was some pain, though I was so numb that there was less than I expected. And when it was over, Greg was delighted with himself. He had experienced something he wanted and had no concept of how emotionally damaging his actions could be.

I told my mother what happened and she was irate. She warned Greg that if he ever touched me like that again, she would have him thrown in jail.

I was shocked. I knew that he had raped me but I couldn't see why she talked of jail. Greg was my friend, my only friend.

For the first time one of the patterns of the kept woman had emerged for me. I would tolerate the intolerable rather than lose the only secure male figure in my life. My father had seduced and abandoned me, though I continued to fantasize that he would return. None of my stepfathers had been close to me, my current stepfather being a violent man, out of control from drink. Greg was an older man who had shown an interest in both me and my future. I would accept the rape rather than risk losing him.

To add to the emotional impact of the experience, I broke up with my boyfriend. I was determined to have a career in show business. He was equally determined to have a wife who stayed home to raise the children. There was growing tension between the two of us until he left to attend school in Arizona, effectively ending the relationship.

Not long after this period, my mother entered the hospital for an operation. My stepfather, though alcoholic and abusive, did love his wife and was unable to cope effectively with the fact of her illness. He was scared, hiding in the bottle until he became so drunk that he was out of control. When I tried to talk with him, he struck me across the face.

I did not realize it but I had subconsciously established standards I would follow as a kept woman. My face was going to be my fortune. This I was already discovering through the beauty contests. A man could strike me but he had to respect my face. I would tolerate almost any abuse except something that would alter my looks. When my stepfather crossed the line I had not realized I had drawn, I left the house and walked the several miles it took for me to reach Greg's shop. He had raped me, but he was my friend as well. He had also only wrestled with me, respecting my body in an almost perverted manner. If I could no longer live at home, perhaps Greg would take me in.

Greg was thrilled with what he saw to be his conquest. He would groom me for the beauty contests and he would groom me for his personal enjoyment. I did not realize that I was about to become Cinderella and he was to be my first Prince Charming.

My life moved swiftly. I won the Miss Los Angeles contest, then competed in the Miss World contest. At the time, the winner in Los Angeles was given the same respect as the winner of a state contest. Although I did not win the Miss World contest, I was asked by one of the men involved, a man who was one of the wealthiest men in the Philippines, if I would travel the world with several of the other girls. We would have all our expenses paid, be given fabulous gifts, and gain international exposure. I readily agreed.

But before the travels could take place, the man, Rodrigo (for political reasons his real name cannot be used here), asked me to accompany him to an extremely expensive hotel. There we would each have our own separate suite where I could enjoy all the expensive gifts he would buy me. I agreed, dining, drinking, and dancing with him until quite late, then going to my suite in his limousine. Once inside, I locked the door and went to bed.

It was no more than an hour later when I awakened to discover

Rodrigo in my room. He had obtained an extra key, then come to make love to me, thinking that I understood that this was an expected part of the evening. I began screaming at him, my voice rising to a pitch where he realized I was becoming hysterical. He backed away and returned to his own suite. I gathered my gifts, found the limousine driver, and convinced him to take me back home. I called Rodrigo, using the car telephone, and explained that I had to go back. I thought he would cancel the trip for me, but he accepted what had happened and continued the plans to take me around the world.

And so it began. Greg raped me, yet showed that he cared by giving me a home. Rodrigo backed away from what he hoped would be a sexual seduction, showering me with presents both before and after the attempt. Love meant gifts and love occasionally meant violence. Cinderella was to be pampered. Cinderella was to be pursued. Life was to be one ball after another. And if "happily ever after" did not appear right away, maybe it would be there tomorrow. Or so I fantasized.

I was one of the luckier kept women in that I had the option of independence. There was a brief marriage to Greg, the birth of a baby, then the traumatic loss of my child to Sudden Infant Death syndrome. This was followed by a career that included having major modeling assignments and a contract as one of the Max Factor girls, becoming the spokesperson for Mexican tourism, and eventually being one of the highest-paid fashion models in the world. Yet always there was the obsession with my father, an obsession that I reinforced at the age of twenty after I briefly returned to where he lived following work in two low-budget movies.

I went to seduce him. I had been in therapy for a couple of years because of the trauma of the baby and the emotional upheaval with my family. I think that's the only reason I didn't go to bed with him.

To my surprise, I discovered that my father had maintained scrapbooks of my career. Although he lived in a different state, he had clippings of my triumphs in the beauty contests, reviews of my films, and copies of my advertisements. I had changed my name when I had begun to be successful, choosing one that was easier to pronounce, but this had not kept him from following my career.

I stayed in his house, hoping he'd come into my bedroom. Each night before I went to sleep, I carefully applied my makeup so I would look perfect. Then, to protect it from being damaged while I slept, I put on a model's mask. This is a zippered hood that fits over your head and face to protect the makeup when you are putting on or taking off clothing while on an assignment. Wearing it to bed preserved the makeup, but I never thought of what I must have looked like as I slept.

I must have looked like a Martian from outer space. If my father had come into the room while I had the mask on, he probably would have been scared to death. But I never thought of that. I just wanted to have perfect makeup for him. Fortunately for both of us he never came in.

We went to a bar together, just like old times. Only this time I wasn't two years old. I wore a leopard coat and had a great figure. I put my hand on his knee, squeezing it at times and rubbing my hand on his thigh. I wanted to arouse him and I was doing it.

Then, when we got home, we kissed and it wasn't a father-daughter kiss. It was obvious to me that I had him. I could take off his clothes and go to bed with him. He was mine, not anyone else's. And that's when I stopped.

I didn't need anything else. I had to know that I could go to bed with him but I didn't actually have to do it. The knowledge was enough. I left shortly thereafter and didn't see him again for years.

The near incestuous relationship later proved to be a family pattern. My father lived with his mother between marriages and she always stayed in the same city where he was living. After her death, it became fairly evident that she had controlled her son through incestuous sex. He was just following the pattern he had been taught when growing up.

I eventually spent more than twenty years as a kept woman, going from man to man to man. My sense of self-worth came from riding in Rolls-Royces, limousines, and private jets. I traveled the world, willing to turn down any job if a man offered me a mansion in which to live, servants, and lavish parties. Sometimes I would refuse to have sex with the man, feeling in control of the relationship when I denied him what he wanted. At other times I was a participant in whatever he desired, from oral sex to bringing another woman into bed. Some of the men were violent, giving me beatings I tolerated so long as they did not mar my face. Other men were passive, putting me on a pedestal to be adored but never understood.

I was not proud of what I did or allowed the men to do to me. I feel sick about admitting to my past, frightened by what others might think of me. It was not a delightful, amorous adventure. It was a life of quiet desperation where I never let anyone, including myself, witness the true feelings seething inside. Had I truly looked at myself, I am not certain that I could have gone on. I was not ready to face my past, to try to understand my mother and the stress she had undergone, or to learn whether or not I had the potential to do more than run from man to man, always fleeing commitment and any chance for self-respect.

The men with whom I spent my time were often neurotic individuals, desperately seeking a reminder of their youth. They liked their women brilliant, beautiful, and with the lack of sophistication found only in the young. The women they sought were barely of legal age. A woman reaching her twenty-fourth birthday was a woman who could be discarded. As a result, I spent sixteen years claiming that I was only twenty-four until finally I had to admit that I had become too well known, too familiar, too "old" to be a play toy for the men.

The realization that I was an addict who needed to break the habit came in a brutal series of incidents that forced me to face the truth about myself.

I was forty in a world where players in their twenties were overage. I had come to recognize that I was addicted to a highly destructive life-style. Increasingly I had been involved with men who were violent toward me, yet with whom I continued to associate. I retained photographs of myself from when I was a top international model. I framed a letter from the office of a major presidential adviser. I talked of what was happening in Monte Carlo, Cannes, Rome, London, Paris, and other sections of the world, but I was speaking of past trips, past associations. The telephone no longer rang with offers for the modeling jobs I once dominated. The men who contacted me were fewer in number, less sophisticated than in the past, no longer the world's elite. My prime was past and I knew it.

I had been in contact with my mother and stepfather, but their relationship was strained. I retained the love-hate relationship with my mother that had been fostered by the father who had abandoned our family. I had never established an adult relationship with my mother, retaining the anger and feelings of rebellion that had fueled my adolescence. We women had shared more than we realized, yet we could not communicate effectively with each other. I looked upon my mother as a last resort in life, someone to whom I would turn only when the world, as I knew it, had come to an end. And, frighteningly, that end was drawing near.

The first realization I faced was that I had nothing to show for my years of high income and high living. Having my own money was never important to me because money meant independence and independence meant an absence of love. It was important to spend my money as fast as I could, not retaining any for personal use. If I made a purchase for myself, it could not have intrinsic worth because such items were assets and assets, again, meant freedom. Thus I might buy an expensive dress or a pair of shoes, but I dared not purchase antiques, rare coins, mutual-fund shares, or real estate. What I preferred to purchase were items for the men who kept me, simultaneously pleasing them and assuring I would have no money of my own.

One of the men who kept me smoked a pipe, so everywhere I traveled, I bought him the most expensive pipes I could find. Some of them were apparently quite valuable, but I didn't care. I just had to please him.

Each new romance brought hope. We're going to Scottsdale, Arizona, to buy a new Rolls-Royce, I would announce happily when talking of one of the men who was keeping me. We're going to Hawaii for a few days to rest on the beach.

The talk sounded enthusiastic, but there was an underlying feeling of fear and pain. I had owned my own business at one time, a period when I had married the man who was keeping me. But he contracted a fatal, expensive disease and eventually I lost everything, including the sense of self that would have enabled me to become a successful businessperson on my own. I had to cling to any man who wanted me, like an aging call girl who, each year, finds herself working from less and less reputable hotels.

The man who took me to the Rolls-Royce dealer in Arizona began to beat me. When I was forced to leave his company, I had all my possessions in a few suitcases and nothing else. The personal items I had stored with my mother were the memories of my beginning, the trophies, ribbons, and faded clippings of yesterday's beauty pageants. The most complete scrapbook of my early life was probably the one retained by my father, a man whose interest was incestuous, not parental. In my mind, little of my present life was worth a future memory.

The normal woman does not attain her true beauty until she reaches forty. She needs that time to experience life, to develop the inner strength, the love, the ability to grieve, to laugh, to understand the vast joys and deep sorrows that life holds for us all. Then, though her skin may not be so taut as it was at twenty, her hair may be flecked with white, and the lines on her face still there after a night's rest, her entire being radiates with the inner glow of the survivor who has come to grips with life. When she cries, there is a depth of sorrow the young can not understand, coupled with the awareness that there is also hope for the future because she has experienced other tragedies and lived to welcome the dawn of new and better days. And when she loves, there is a passion that comes from having sampled men in enough sizes, shapes, and personalities to know that this man, the one she has chosen, is not only the right one for her, but the man whom she can trust, to whom she can be vulnerable, to whom she can give heart, soul, and body with complete abandon. But for me being forty was the end of life as I had known it. At least half my physical life lay ahead of me, yet everything I thought I wanted, everything I thought I needed, was being offered only to women half my age.

Then there was another man because there had always been another man. "Use my house, consider my staff your staff, drive my car." It was a familiar litany I heard and I fantasized that all was well again. I was still in the game, still competing with the twenty year olds, still a prize to be won by men who competed for the attention my presence on their arm would bring.

But the man who loaned me his house could not keep me there, did not want me there. He had his own life, his own kept woman. I was no longer his but merely a friend, or perhaps a faded memory for whom he retained enough love or enough guilt to provide what was little more than a few days' vacation.

I was on the streets, living from my car, desperately calling men I knew, yet trying to disguise the panic in my voice.

There was one man, rich, famous, his name in all the gossip columns, his presence desired at all the right parties during the proper seasons in the international cities where the elite liked to play. He had said, "I love you, Leslie. I want to marry you, Leslie. If you will but call, I will take you in my arms, make you my wife, give you anything you want."

But I had not been ready for marriage. Marriage meant love, commitment, mutual respect, all the things that a kept woman felt she did not deserve. What mattered was hearing the proposal, not acting upon it. Until then. Until I was living from my car, having fled one abusive man and been asked to leave the house of a second man who was no longer interested in me.

I called the man, who was thrilled to hear my voice, to know that I would at last fulfill his desires. "Come to me," he told me. "Come to me at once."

And then there was the storybook ending. Cinderella raced to the arms of the Prince. The house was large, well-furnished, familiar. The servants greeted me with kindness. He took me in his arms, embraced me, spoke of love, caring, and the future.

The bags were left behind for the moment. There was so much that had to be said, but not in words. What mattered could be shared only in the bedroom, the touch of two once and future lovers renewing an acquaintance that had too long been on hold.

His hands roamed my body, bringing pleasure, comfort, safety. I was at once a small child being cuddled by the father I cherished, feeling safe from all the lonely fears of life, and also an adult woman needing a lover's erection probing my body, each thrust saying, "I love you. I want you. You're mine."

And then it was over, his passion spent, our bodies covered with a sheen of perspiration. "I'm so glad you came, Leslie. But I really must ask you to leave because I have some extremely important work to do. Let me give you a hundred dollars for gas. I know you had to drive a long way over here."

Shocked, horrified, wanting to scream and scream until there was no more breath in me, I smiled the gay, delighted smile I had learned to put on my face like another item of makeup when I had been a world-class model. I expressed my thanks, my pleasure at being with him, and returned to my car, frightened by the fact that I had kept the money he gave me.

But wait. There was another man, equally rich, equally famous, equally caring. I placed a call from a telephone booth, heard the words I had heard from the other man just hours earlier. The difference was that this time they were said with sincerity. I could tell that from the tone of his voice. There would be no more hurt, no more pain. I drove to him quickly, wondering why I had not called him in the first place.

I did not realize at first that I was living an instant replay of my life as recorded by a sadistic videographer working for a news crew trained in hell. It was only when I was again lying in bed, basking in this man's arms, that the words he too was saying worked through to my conscious mind. "A hundred dollars." "Gas money." "Drove a long way to get here."

Gone was the kept woman who captivated the men of Monte Carlo. Gone was the world-famous model in her early twenties who had the cosmetics account, the magazine covers, the photographers vying for the chance to pay her exorbitant fees.

By any standards other than those of the perverted world of kept women and the men who keep them, I was a beautiful woman, intelligent, capable of learning and doing anything I desired. But I did not understand that life could be lived without yachts, private helicopters, and freely flowing champagne. The real world offers beauty, pleasure, respect, and hope, yet kept women can see the real world only through the distorted glass of a fun-house mirror. I was a part of a sick minority, so carefully insulated that I thought I was part of the majority, and the majority had rejected me. I had been forsaken by the movers and shakers in international politics and high finance, and in my mind, at that moment, such abandonment was worse than being forsaken by God.

There was a third call, an honest one, a plea for help. The man was in real estate, owning some of the most expensive retail land in the United States.

The man told me that he had a business meeting that would last until ten P.M. He told me where it would be held and asked me to meet him in the parking lot of a shopping area. The stores sold extremely expensive merchandise, the shopping area was heavily patrolled, and there would be no problems. He knew my car and would come to me as soon as the meeting was over.

There was more a sense of resignation than of hope that I felt about his answer to my call. The man was a friend, for so he had stated many times in the past. He would help me, care for me, give me time to heal from the emotional traumas of the last twenty-four hours.

Ten o'clock came, then passed, but I was not concerned. A man did not become rich by staying with an arbitrary schedule during a business meeting. A delay meant that things were either going very well or very poorly, and either circumstance would keep him from me longer than he had planned.

Ten-thirty passed. The parking lot was empty as the last of the stores' employees left for the night. Security personnel would be on patrol until morning so there was no cause for concern. I was safe and he would be coming.

Eleven o'clock. I fought a growing uneasiness by forcing myself to relax. I closed my eyes, controlled my breathing, tried not to think.

Eleven-thirty. I had dozed for a moment, becoming stiff and cramped in the one position. I shifted my body and looked around, seeing only neon emptiness and the painted eyes of mannequins staring vacantly from store display windows.

Midnight.

One o'clock. I fought the tears because tears would damage my makeup and admitting to emotions was not part of the "game" of being kept.

Two o'clock. I slept, jerked awake, shifted, and slept some more. There was nothing else to do. Nowhere else to turn.

By daylight I knew the truth I had not wished to face. The man was not coming to rescue me. The Cinderella I thought myself to be had run out of Prince Charmings. There were going to be no more balls, no more opportunities to wear the glass slippers. I had an older car, suitcases filled with clothing and makeup, no job, no savings, and no home. All I could do was call my mother and ask for a place to stay.

There is a rather bitter sentiment that says, "Home is the place where you always return because they have to take you in." I was given my old room, could see again some of the trophies of my past. Life, as I once had known it, was over, and too many years seemed to lie ahead. I felt that I had died emotionally and wondered if I should destroy my physical being in acknowledgment of my newfound awareness.

4

Sex and the Kept Woman

Invariably the kept life-style comes down to male-female relationships. Whether a woman experiences a positive kept relationship or she is plunged into the dark, addictive reality experienced by other kept women, the sex act is more than just a means to achieve physical pleasure. It is the first and last area where the participants are able to exert their control over each other. Sex is a dance where each partner alternately leads and follows, a fact that makes it an important area to understand.

I never wanted to write this chapter. Or, more to the point, I never wanted to live it. Sex, for me, has always meant pain, the lust of the emotionally disturbed baby-sitter who molested me, the drooling, incestuous insanity of my grandfather, the violent, self-centered passion of my first husband. I never knew pleasure from an act that should be the most fulfilling two human beings can experience together. I saw my body as a carrot on a stick, to be dangled in front of a man in order to lead him in whatever direction I wanted to go.

Listening to other women discuss their sex lives was extremely uncomfortable for me. Some knew only pain, often greater than any I imagined possible, and their stories only reinforced my nightmares of the past. Yet some knew pleasure, a physical experience greater than any I thought possible. I did not understand what they were saying, could not share their experience, and was uncomfortable listening to them.

Even now, as this is being written, I am amazed by the stories being recorded. There was so much and such graphic detail that it was obvious that only by discussing what they had either sought or endured could the women put it in perspective for themselves.

The cases described here are typical. We decided to use examples that reflected only what were consistent experiences for at least several of the women. We wanted to show the patterns that kept women were encountering, avoiding the experiences that seemed unique, either unusually pleasurable or unusually bad, yet always varying widely from what were commonly repeated themes.

Some are rather graphic, though we have tried to avoid giving too much detail. What you will be reading are the typical patterns Ted and I heard during the many interviews we conducted both separately and together. The important point is that, in the end, being kept, or keeping a woman, comes down to sex. It may be an angry response. It may be gentle and loving. It may be a sham, with the woman serving as an image that belies the impotency of the seemingly powerful man whose arm she is grasping. And so, uncomfortable or not, the following reflects the experiences we discovered.

Understanding Sex

The sex act can be the most pleasurable act in which a man and woman can engage or it can be the most vicious. The French sometimes call a woman's orgasm *la petite morte*, "the little death." Some American men refer to the penis as a weapon, the owner being a "swordsman." A man can achieve an erection when aroused by great tenderness, yet he also becomes erect during times of both extreme fear and extreme anger. There are sexual addicts who seek sex several times a day, both with a partner and through masturbation. And there are controllers, both men and women who feel that by getting a member of the opposite sex into bed, they no longer have to respect the person. They may protest that they "like men" or "like women," but the reality is that they are using sex to dominate the situation. They view the person who yields to their touch as someone who is weak, no longer worthy of respect.

Another form of domination occurs when a kept woman is shared among men in the same social circle. Usually she is drawn to the unofficial leader of the group, the man who is the wealthiest, most powerful, and/or most respected.

Depending upon the man and the woman involved, the same type of sex act can be loving, gentle, and desired with one couple, and a means of domination, pain, and/or humiliation with another. The women we interviewed told of every possible variation of the sex act, from a woman's refusing to have sex in order to be viewed as a more elusive prize to be captured, to her allowing the man to debase her, agreeing to anything he wanted so long as he would not turn her away. Some women spoke of bondage as a preliminary to the greatest sensual pleasures they had ever known. Others spoke of seemingly the same act as a prelude to the most vicious violence they had ever imagined experiencing in their worst nightmares. There were women who told of dressing in a variety of ways to enhance the man's excitement, and there were those who told of costumes meant to help the men relate to fantasy women for whom they would feel no emotions. Some participated in the pleasurable variations discussed in such best sellers as *The Joy of Sex*. Others spoke of experiences that implied the men learned their sexual foreplay from the Marquis de Sade.

But always sex had a purpose. For some it was to feel good, because "I deserve the best. I deserve to be treated like a queen. I deserve a man who will do anything I want to my body until I decide whether or not I want him in me."

For others it was a way to ensure they would not have to leave the man and go out in the "real world." "If he wanted me to give head to some of his friends while he watched, what was the big deal? All cocks look the same to me no matter how big some guy says his is." "Sure he likes to get a little rough. But he never touches my face and he always buys me a new dress, slips me some money, goes on this guilt-trip thing afterward where I can do no wrong, you know? For what he gives me to spend, I guess I can put up with a little roughhouse. It's not much worse than playing football with my brothers when I was growing up, you know?"

In some instances the man involved has achieved so high a position of power, money, and/or status that the woman will tolerate anything he does. She fantasizes that it is his busy schedule that causes him to do things quickly, seemingly without emotional involvement. She views his erection as an outward, visible sign of his commitment to her, his love, as it were, becoming aroused and ready to receive her even though she will become but another statistic to him. Her name and face will be vague memories, the aroma of her perfume, the differences in her touch, the contours of her body, all blending together into a meaningless conglomeration. Yet she neither knows this reality nor would believe it if it were told to her.

The Power Lovers

President John Kennedy was probably the most widely known power figure who had both what he called "fucks" and women who were essentially "kept," such as Judith Campbell Exner, who later wrote a kiss-and-tell book. Kennedy bragged to his brother-in-law, the late actor Peter Lawford, that he liked to have a woman "three different ways before he was done with her." Former Secret Service men assigned to the White House told how Kennedy would often have sex with at least two different women a day, not counting his wife. Yet there was no foreplay, no thought to the woman's pleasure.

The late actress Marilyn Monroe was one of Kennedy's most intense relationships, so intense that Marilyn thought he would divorce Jackie, marry her, and she would be first lady during the second term in the White House. Yet though she fantasized that Jack truly loved her, she confided to both Peter and columnist Jim Bacon, among others, that Kennedy was "lousy" in bed. There was no foreplay, no sensitivity. The appeal was that he wanted her, would give her a position and respectability that she coveted. She would tolerate his neglect because of the gain she expected. When she learned that she was considered just another "fuck," she twice overdosed on sleeping pills, the second time not being caught before the medication took her life.

Oddly, there are men who have even less sensitivity to women than Kennedy did who achieve a reputation as great lovers. The most humorous story was told by Janelle, who decided to have a one-night stand with a man whose reputation was that of being the greatest lover in Hollywood. Janelle wondered to what heights of ecstasy his loving touch would guide her. She anticipated pleasure more intense than any romantic novel. What she experienced made her wonder about the skills of whatever press agent had established his image as a sexual being.

"It began over dinner in London," Janelle relates. "I was traveling with Sam Spiegel, the producer of such movies as *On the Waterfront, Bridge on the River Kwai, Lawrence of Arabia,* and *Nicholas and Alexandra,* among others. We had left his yacht in order to dine with the actor, whom I'll call Henry, his live-in girlfriend, Samantha, and two other people, an entertainer and his wife.

"As always with Sam, the meal was flawless. We started with a 1948 Chateau Lafite-Rothschild, a red wine that costs hundreds of dollars a bottle, then ate lightly—broiled whitefish and salad for me, angel hair pasta for the entertainer, and similar orders for the others. It was what I had come to know as the typical jet set meal: high protein, low carbohydrate, and a bill for the six of us that approached a thousand dollars. What made the meal unusual was the fact that it led to a brief, intense, and ultimately hilarious romantic encounter with the most charismatic actor I had ever met.

"We had just sat down for dinner in the private dining area of a small London restaurant. I remember looking in awe at Henry, the actor/producer who became famous for movies that sometimes were extraordinarily violent and other times were remarkably sensitive. He was also known as one of the great lovers in Hollywood, a man who had had relationships with what seemed like every young leading lady in the film industry. The night we met he was with his live-in, one of the most beautiful women I have ever seen. I was just twenty-six and, though a successful model, I felt that there was no way my appearance could compare with hers.

"As the first glasses of wine were poured, I suddenly felt my leg being touched under the table. Then I realized that Henry had wrapped himself around me in such a way that I could remove my foot only by lifting my leg in such a way that it would call attention to what was happening.

"At first I was naïve enough to think it was an accident. Henry was not looking at me in any special way. His live-in certainly did not notice what was taking place, and I could tell by looking at Sam that he was oblivious. Then Henry began grasping my ankle and releasing it, grasping and releasing it, the moves obviously meant to gain my attention.

"I was startled, yet unable to say anything. My relationship with Sam was strictly one of being kept in Europe. He was paying for my trip, providing me with private suites and the finest food while I served as his escort everywhere. But there was no sex. He understood that I had a boyfriend back in California at the time, a relationship that had been extremely troubled of late, yet one to which I wanted to remain faithful.

"Suddenly I was receiving a rather blatant signal that one of the most exciting actors in the world was interested in me. Even more, he was risking his relationship with the beautiful woman who was sitting next to him. I was scared, annoyed, and flattered simultaneously.

"The meal progressed without anyone's noticing. Henry's live-in was trying to gain a part in Sam Spiegel's next movie, and I divided my conversation between Henry and the actors. Sam made some comment about my trying for the film, but I had no interest in a movie career at that time, a fact that was obvious to his live-in. She saw me as no threat and apparently never realized the game Henry was playing under the table.

"When the dinner was over, Henry hugged me, then left with Samantha. Sam and I returned to the hotel where, as usual, a single, flawless rose, a bottle of white wine, and a basket of fresh fruit had been left for me. Sam was the last of the Hollywood mogul era and he knew how to treat a woman. I also had a telephone call from my boyfriend back in Los Angeles, but when I returned it, he was out with another woman. I was irate with him, still thinking of Henry, and not certain what to do next when the telephone rang.

" 'Janelle, this is Henry,' said the voice on the telephone. 'I have to be with you.'

"I said something meaningless about Sam, but Henry knew that we were not sharing a room together.

" 'Don't you see, Janelle? It's our destiny. I've met a lot of women in my time. You know that. You see me in the papers with so many different women. But never have I felt fated to be with someone. Never have I entered a room and known that our being together was a destiny neither of us could fight.

" 'We are so much alike, Janelle, you and me. We are as one, though we have never been together before.'

"I sat on the bed, listening to a line that sounded like it had been created by a teenager suffering from equal parts of excess hormones and too many trashy novels. Yet Henry, the male sex symbol of the

American movie industry, was using it on me. Perhaps if the circumstances had been different I would have told him off. But I was not living in a world of reality. Sam Spiegel, one of the most successful producers of the past twenty years, was so enamored with me that he wanted me traveling with him. My boyfriend was being unfaithful, a sure sign that our relationship was over. And now Henry had left the glamorous Samantha in order to attempt to seduce me with one of the corniest lines I had ever heard. I decided that for once in my life I was going to live a fantasy other women can only imagine.

" 'You must meet me for a drink. Just a drink, Janelle. I want nothing else from you. We have so little time. For all we know, this may be the only moment in our lives, the one instant in all eternity when we can get together. We must share this moment. We must yield to our destiny and have a drink.'

"It was all too ridiculous. 'No, Henry,' I said. 'I'm tired, it's been a long evening already, and the hotel bar is just too small for anything discreet. Thank you, Henry, and good night.'

"It was late the next morning when the hotel telephone rang again. Henry had discovered an Oriental restaurant one block from the hotel. 'We are going to meet there, Janelle. You are going to go to the bar and we are going to have a drink; one drink. No one will see us. No one will know. And to do otherwise is to deny the destiny that is ours. You cannot say no. Now hurry for I will be there in twenty minutes.'

"I cursed the arrogance of the man, then rationalized the rendezvous. I wanted this nuttiness. I wanted to be flattered by his attention. And I knew that there was no harm in a single drink. I quickly changed clothes and went to the bar.

"Henry and I began talking. 'There's one thing I have to know, Henry,' I said. 'Why me last night? You had that beautiful girl with you, so why were you playing with my feet under the table?'

"Henry seemed stunned by my question. 'Don't you know who you are, Janelle? Don't you see how much alike we are? It was our destiny to meet. It was an experience beyond our control.'

"We drank a little, then Henry suddenly gave me an address and some money for a cab. 'You are going to meet me at Roman Polanski's flat. Here's the address. I'm using it while he's away and you are to meet me at four o'clock this afternoon. It has taken who knows how many eons of lifetimes for us to come together like this. It is our destiny to be together this afternoon. Be there, Janelle.' And with that, he was gone. There was no time to think, to say no, to do anything except laugh at the utter ridiculousness of the situation. I also knew I would go.

"Roman Polanski's apartment outside looked a little like a New York town house. The interior was rather stark, everything done in black and white, with minimal decorations adorning the walls. What was unusual was the furniture, perhaps the most shocking I had ever seen.

"First there was the coffee table. The base was a hand-carved figure of a naked woman, her body arched backward so that the glass top would rest on her knees, crotch, and breasts.

"Then there were the chairs. Again, each was shaped like a woman, this time seated. The arms were the arms of a woman and your back rested against her breasts. It seemed the type of furniture you might have if you were a horny sixteen year old with an unlimited source of money and highly tolerant parents. The fact that Roman Polanski was an internationally known producer who had also been the husband of Sharon Tate, one of the Manson family murder victims, made the situation rather distasteful.

"I'm not certain what I expected when I arrived, but I did think there would be a romantic setting. Perhaps there would be a fireplace or a bottle of fine champagne properly chilled. There would undoubtedly be flowers and perhaps some caviar to eat. Music would be included, playing unobtrusively in the background. Certainly we would talk, kiss a bit, and then, when the mood was right, quietly adjourn to the bedroom for a slow, sensual, rapturous experience. It would be casual sex, of course, though the sensations would linger in my memory for decades to come. I would be seduced by one of the grand masters. Or so I thought.

" 'Come upstairs, Janelle,' said Henry, taking my hand and pulling me to the staircase. I was wearing a sweater and black leather pants, the sweater an obstacle he was determined to remove as we climbed to the second floor.

" 'Henry, please, can't you wait?' I asked, resisting his pulling at me.

" 'You know why we're here. Just let me get it off.'

"I continued to resist and then decided against it. I had come here to experience whatever was going to take place. Pulling off my sweater on the way up the stairs seemed a little crude, but that was not the point. I wanted to experience whatever Henry wanted to do and if that included stripping me half-naked on the way up, so be it.

"The bedroom was as stark as the rest of the house. The bed was a contemporary design with a chrome-metal arching bar at the base. The ceiling was mirrored and I had the distinct impression that there was a hidden camera, tape recorder, or both somewhere. I also didn't care.

"Henry stripped our clothes from both of our bodies, had me lie down, and entered me without any foreplay. I was not ready for him and his entrance was uncomfortable, yet I said nothing. This was his show and I was going along for the ride.

"Suddenly Henry hooked his feet on the chrome bar, placed his hands on the bed on either side of my body, and, his erection firmly planted inside my vagina, began doing push-ups. 'You'll love this,' he said, but he was not talking to me. He was looking up at the mirror, periodically repositioning himself so he could see himself better.

" 'This is great sex, really great sex,' he said, still not speaking to me. The push-ups grew faster, more intense. 'We're so much alike. So glad we got together. Our destiny, really. Fate brought us together. So glad. Great sex. Really great sex.'

"And then I started to laugh. The sex symbol of the Western world was making love like a character from a Peter Sellers movie. I had no sexual feelings, no pleasure at all. In fact, I wondered why I was there, other than to be a convenient receptacle while he sexually massaged his ego.

"My body shook with laughter, tears coming to my eyes. If Henry noticed, he probably thought the laughter was my way of achieving orgasm. He just kept doing the push-ups faster and faster until he climaxed, then he withdrew and seemed to leap to the floor.

" 'I told you it was our destiny, Janelle. We're so much alike. Wasn't it great sex?' He was prancing about the floor, seemingly as happy as if he had just won the Academy Award for one of his pictures.

"If I had been the type to keep a diary of my experiences during those early years, that night, upon making my entry concerning my amorous adventure with one of America's great sex symbols, I would have lied."

Perhaps the most amusing sex was no sex at all. This occurred with a man who was once one of the most powerful individuals in Washington. He was an adviser to presidents, worked with foreign heads of state, and regularly traveled the world.

Ken met Angelique at a party given by a wealthy businessman in South America. Ken traveled with bodyguards because of his importance to the government, but he was able to relax at the party since it was a private affair, not a matter of diplomacy. He became intrigued with Angelique because she was both bright and naïve. She had no idea who he was or of his importance, nor did she care. She found him fascinating for his intellect and the two of them discussed a wide range of subjects of mutual interest, none of which related to politics.

Later there would be other involvement, including Angelique providing Ken with a horoscope she had made for him. Whether or not he believed in such matters as astrology, he was delighted by what, for him, was a most unusual gift and he was fascinated by reading it.

Angelique was Ken's guest at a dinner at the White House and there were periods of travel during the year she was involved with him. But the relationship, for a number of reasons, never proved sexual. And, in the world in which Ken traveled, to not have sex with a beautiful woman could result in whispers that perhaps the man was impotent or even homosexual, neither of which was true as Ken proved with the women he married before and after his involvement with Angelique. Yet Ken could not risk such hints of scandal.

"Ken came with me to my hotel room after one date," Angelique explained. "Secret Service agents had accompanied us that night, remaining discreetly at a distance and staying outside the room which, I assume, had previously had a security check. Anyway, Ken and I said good night, but instead of leaving the room, Ken took the day's paper, stretched out on the bed, and read it front to back. Then he checked his watch, decided that we would have had enough time for sex, and rose to go. When I asked him why he had done that, he smiled and said, 'I have to maintain my reputation with the Secret Service.' "

Men wanting sexual variations was a repeated theme among the women we interviewed, almost always married men. It was as though the men had married women whose moneyed backgrounds, social positions, and/or educations (often in exclusive private schools or strict parochial ones) had made them wary of any variation from normal (the missionary position) intercourse. The men had either suggested something different and been repulsed, or they had been afraid to express their desires. Whatever the circumstance, they recognized the vulnerability of a kept woman. They knew that she might share the perceived pleasure of their fantasies. In other instances they did not care about the woman's reaction. She wanted to ride in a Rolls-Royce, party on a yacht, fly in a private jet, and live in a spare house, and the men knew that such desires would override any thought of protest against what they were suggesting.

"What drew me to Philippe was the way he wanted me to have pleasure in bed," said Carla. She was twenty-three, a model who was working in Paris. He was fifty-one and referred to himself as a "shop-keeper." In reality, he owned expensive boutiques in Rome, Paris, London, New York, and Beverly Hills, in addition to being of royal blood. His connection to royalty meant less in modern-day France, but the inheritance from that connection was worth millions.

"I had never had sex with a man like that," said Carla. "I started modeling when I was thirteen, and I was making over two hundred dollars an hour before I was a junior in high school. There was a level you reach where you might be better than the other girls competing, but you can't prove that unless you get the right job with the right photographer and magazine. I discovered that if I would occasionally have sex with someone—not very often, mind you, but at the right time with the right man—I could get those jobs and show what I could do. Then I'd move up the scale a little higher, reach another of those plateaus, and do it again.

"It didn't matter about the man's age or his looks. There was some-thing exciting about being wanted, adored, yet knowing I was in control. The fact that most of them wanted a quickie on a couch in their office or maybe to spend the night at some fancy hotel after first having the most elaborate meal room service would bring up did not matter to me. I got used to casual sex that wasn't very satisfying at times but certainly was financially rewarding.

"Philippe was different. He bought me gifts. He set me up with my own apartment so I would have some place permanent when I was in Paris for an assignment. He said that hotels were too impersonal. He did not say that he also had a key to the apartment, something I learned by accident because he never abused that fact. He never let himself in that I knew about and he only stayed the night when I invited him.

"Philippe wanted to experiment with me. He wanted to know what gave me pleasure. He wanted to discover what would relax me and what would get me aroused. One time he gave me a bubble bath, washing my hair, massaging my back and neck, stroking my legs and gently bringing me to orgasm as I lay back in the tub, my eyes closed, my head resting on a plastic cushion just above the water.

"I kept saying, 'How can I please you? What excites you?' But all he'd say was that seeing me happy, relaxed, and wanting him brought him all the happiness he needed.

"'I felt guilty, though. I told him that he was too good to me, that I should be doing something to make him happy. It was my responsibility to please him as he was pleasing me.

"Philippe looked at me mischievously. He asked me to repeat what I had said and I told him that it was my responsibility to please him. He just nodded and said he would see me that night.

"I could tell something special was happening then. He arrived wearing a tuxedo and told me we were going some place special. He took me to what must have been the most expensive restaurant in Paris. The music came from a twenty-piece orchestra. The food was made of elaborate ingredients and was given an exquisite presentation. The champagne cost more than the meal and the meal cost more than most Parisians earn in a month. We ate and drank to satisfaction, then danced until we were delightfully giddy. Finally we returned to my apartment, where I knew he would be spending the night.

"When we got out of the car, he took a small bag from the backseat. Then, when we got settled inside, he looked at me with the same mischievous grin. 'A woman should not be responsible for sexual pleasure,' Phillipe said to me. 'The man should get pleasure from her enjoyment of his touch.' Then he kissed me and I suddenly realized he was tying my hands behind my back with a length of rope he had carried in the bag.

"I was frightened by his actions, especially when he made certain it was secure enough so I could not get loose. He had me sit on the couch, then tied my ankles together. Then he went into the bedroom and came out with one of my scarves which he tied over my mouth. The gag was loose enough so I could probably have talked, but I was getting excited by what was happening and didn't want to stop him. This was a side of Philippe I had not seen before, and though I was scared, I wanted him to do whatever he was going to do.

"He started slowly. His hands went to my back, working the muscles in my shoulders. I was positioned awkwardly, yet it still felt wonderful as he kneaded the skin.

"Then he gradually undressed me, stroking my face, my arms, my legs, until he had to untie my wrists in order to get everything off. I started to reach for the gag, but he made me stop. He told me that I was to have no responsibility for anything that happened. I was to be silent and just experience his touch.

"He retied my wrists in front of me, then freed my legs so he could finish removing my clothing. Then he took me into the bedroom, picked me up, and laid me on the bed, propping the pillows beneath my head so I could watch him. He retied my ankles, then slowly undressed.

"You have to understand something about Philippe. He's not a particularly attractive man. He has a small potbelly. He's balding oddly, with some of his hair receding in front, some of it coming out in the back, so there is a patch that looks a little like a Buddhist monk's. I mean, he's not like the men who work at Chippendale's [nightclubs featuring male strippers]. Yet there was something about what he was doing, touching me, taking off his clothes for me, tying me up so I had no responsibility for anything that happened . . . I don't think I've ever been so sexually aroused in my life.

"I don't know how long he touched me. He kept shifting my body, sometimes having me on my stomach, other times on my back, never letting me free any longer than I had to be so he could reposition me in comfort. He avoided touching my genitals and that got me even more excited. I found myself straining against the bonds, wanting to grab him, to have him inside me.

"Then he freed my mouth and I began begging him to enter. He kissed me, exploring my mouth with his tongue. And then he worked his way down my body, sucking my nipples, kissing my breasts, my stomach, my pubic hair . . .

"I was ready to scream when he entered me. He had freed my ankles but he didn't undo my wrists until he was inside me and then all I could do was grab his back and hold on. I can't describe the feelings. It was a little like the aftershock waves of one of the bigger earthquakes we've had out here or maybe the way that vibrator they have in some hotel room beds—Magic Fingers, I think it's called—feels, only inside of me, not outside.

"I know he had fun. His face was flush and he was beaming from ear to ear when he finally caught his breath. But what was exciting was that he had done it for me, refused to let me feel responsible for the pleasuring, wanted me to feel something I've never felt before. No man was ever like that. It was always 'make *me* feel good, baby!'

"I don't think I was in love with Philippe. Not a serious

commitment. But it was like I was addicted to the sex. I wanted to ride in the Rolls. I wanted the apartment, the nice meals. And maybe that's why I let him do that to me. I mean, I wasn't into anything kinky like that before. Maybe I let him do it because I didn't want to lose those other things. I just know that he didn't want to hurt me. He could have done anything to me and all he did was keep building those feelings inside me.

"God, if I ever find someone like Philippe who's single, younger, and wants me like that . . . The Rolls isn't all that important. The money wouldn't matter. I find someone who wants me like that who's single and will bring out those feelings . . . I'll stay with him forever."

Carla was fortunate. Philippe wanted her to have pleasure and her desires matched the ways in which he wanted to enjoy sex. They were two consenting adults exploring ways to increase sexual tension and pleasurable release. Linda was not so fortunate. She discovered a different world where men play games meant to bring humiliation, pain, and, if they go too far, death.

"We knew the actor's reputation. It was common knowledge around Beverly Hills that he liked abuse," said Mara. "There was even a rumor that he had a mock medieval torture room in the basement of his house.

"I don't know if he controlled his urges or if he knew how far to go with a woman. I knew several he had dated and a few he had kept, and none of them seemed to be obviously bruised or scarred. He was really lavish with presents and he had millions of dollars from his pictures. Maybe he bought them off. I don't know.

"There was this new girl in our group, Linda. We all worked for this publication in Beverly Hills because it was a good way to meet the owners and customers of some of the businesses. Many of them were rich and it was a way to get in another kept situation. None of us expected to last in the job, but we were certain it would help us get what we wanted.

"The new girl had been hired as a receptionist with the understanding that she would work into sales. That was what we did because that's where you met the right men.

"Anyway, she was fascinated by our stories. She was so young and innocent—twenty or twenty-one—and she wanted to experience the good life. She had never had champagne or caviar, never snorted cocaine or tried amphetamines. She was thrilled the first time she rode in a Cadillac convertible. It was beyond her imagination to think of a Mercedes, a Lamborghini, or a Rolls. But she wanted to learn . . . God, how she wanted to learn.

"There was a party that was being thrown by one of the clients. It was in a private mansion in the hills and we were all invited, even Linda. She was determined to make a connection with a shah, a prince, or someone else with money, a title, and power like we had been talking about.

"This actor was there, the one we knew was trouble, and Linda was drawn to him. You have to understand how beautiful she was. This was someone who had the looks of one of the old glamour queens of the movies. Her figure was flawless, her face without a blemish, and her hair was naturally healthy with a style that enhanced her looks. She had had offers to model and do commercials, but she didn't want to work that hard. She wanted to meet a man who would take care of her and, I guess, she thought that the party might be her only chance.

"It must have been around eleven when Linda came over to say she was going to another party. The actor said he had a special one going at his place and she'd be perfect for it.

"We tried to talk her out of it. It wasn't that we didn't think that he had a party. It was his reputation. Something didn't feel right about the whole thing and we knew she didn't have the instincts for this kind of thing. She was from a small town and she just . . . She was naïve.

"All we did was get her mad. She thought we were jealous because the actor wasn't interested in us. She thought we didn't know what it was like to be young. And we were so stupid, we didn't keep arguing with her. We watched her go off in his Rolls like she was Cinderella on her way to the ball."

What happened next was learned only indirectly, and then in the day or two between the time Mara saw her in the hospital and the day that Linda died.

There were only men at the actor's mansion, though they were having a party. There was food, liquor, and music being played.

At first everything was normal so far as Linda was concerned. The men seemed unusually friendly, asking her if she was the entertainment for the evening, but she laughed with them, thinking it was friendly teasing. There were drinks and drugs, and she was determined to experience it all.

Finally, unsteady on her feet and no longer thinking clearly, Linda allowed the actor and some of his friends to begin kissing her, fondling her, moving her to another room. She closed her eyes, a smile on her face, as one of the men held her hands high above her head. She felt someone else attach what felt like bracelets, gifts, undoubtedly, from her many admirers. Someone else was fondling her breasts, and she realized he must have gone beneath her blouse and bra. Someone else was touching her legs.

It was all such fun, so innocent, so . . .

The pain was only slightly sobering. She was so heavily drugged and drunk that they were done with her before she realized that two men had entered her simultaneously, one in the vagina, the other in the anus. She started to lower her hands, then discovered that they were in handcuffs that had been suspended from the ceiling.

She later recalled blurred faces, the sting of a lash, objects forced into every body opening, and horrifying screams of terror that, only later, she realized were her own. Eventually she found herself on a bed, her flesh badly swollen, her jaw broken, her body bleeding, too weak to resist or even to cry out.

But by then the men were no longer with her. They had been aroused by her expression of pain. They had been delighted by her screams, by seeing her bonds cut into her flesh as she twisted one way and then another in a desperate attempt to free herself. Once she had become a battered hulk of her former self, unable to do anything but endure, they had abandoned her.

Slowly, painfully, Linda dragged herself from the bed. The men were in a different section of the house, still talking, laughing, drinking. She had been there more than two days, the violence taking place in shifts, but she had no sense of time. They had not kept her in restraints, apparently certain that she would sleep, hopefully recovering enough for another session in a few hours.

Linda managed to get to a telephone, calling her mother, finding an address on a letter discarded on the table where the telephone was resting. Her mother told her to get outside, that she would drive over to get her.

Linda ended up in the hospital where she told what happened to Mara, her mother, and the other girls. They were horrified and terrified at the same time. The men who had beaten Linda were rich and powerful. The women felt that they would not hesitate to kill them if they tried to go to the police. And if they did not kill them, they would bribe the right officials to be certain that none of the information ever resulted in arrests. They told themselves that there was nothing they could do except warn others against such experiences. Even when Linda died in the hospital, they claimed no knowledge of what had happened, reinforcing Linda's story that she had been in a car wreck. None of the staff believed her but there was nothing that could be done.

Linda had discovered the dark side of the kept experience and her friends had found an even greater tragedy within themselves. Their silence reflected the fact that they had sold their souls to ensure they could continue as they had in the past. It was easier to let Linda die unavenged than to accept that they were so desperate for the approval of the men in their lives that they would not speak against even the worst of those who supported the life-style.

When Three or More Are Gathered Together

While the reality of three people in bed may be incomprehensible or even disgusting for many people, the fantasy of two members of the opposite sex lusting after your body is probably one you have enjoyed. It is a fantasy that is the subject of countless books and movies. Two men seek one woman, each vying for her affections. Or one man is pursued by two women, each attempting to cater to his every whim, each trying to show him that she is better than the other.

In film and literature, the eternal triangle generally follows several well-established story lines, one being: One man is suave, perhaps rich in a flashy manner, and always handsome. The second man may be his equal, but usually there is something distinctive about him. Perhaps he is also rich, but his work and life-style are such that he does not flaunt his money. Perhaps each man seems equally brave, yet in a crisis, the man who was previously seen as the lesser of the two suddenly proves the most heroic.

And an angle for a scenario with two women: Perhaps one is scheming to take advantage of the man, not truly loving him yet not letting him see her "evil" side. Perhaps, for any number of reasons, one of the women is wrong for the man even though she is otherwise a perfectly admirable human being (which only the viewer/reader knows). Even worse, the other woman, who would be perfect, does not recognize this fact and so is tempted to abandon her pursuit so he can have the person who he mistakenly thinks is the better woman.

The plot variations are many and they feed on both our fantasies and our insecurities. We might feel that if one man or woman pursues us, then there must be something wrong with that person because we do not feel ourselves worthy of his or her love. But if two members of the opposite sex are in pursuit, then we must be very special indeed.

Such fantasies remain fantasies for the majority of us. Sexual researchers/writers such as Nancy Friday (*My Secret Garden*) have found that many women indulge in fantasies where several men have them helpless, then have sex with them. Generally these fantasies fall in the rape fantasy category, yet the women do not desire to have them acted out. They are a form of stimulating mental foreplay in preparation for sex with a lover or spouse, the only man they truly want engaging in intercourse with them.

Men reportedly share similar fantasies, often involving, for example, attractive women with whom they work or sisters of their wives or lovers. Yet when it comes to actually indulging in sex, they want only a single partner; they too use fantasy as mental foreplay.

A man who keeps a woman has already broken one of society's taboos. He has violated the sanctity of his marriage vows or his spoken commitment to a live-in lover. He has the wealth, the power, and the moral license that allow him to indulge himself in any way he finds amusing. As a result, all the kept women we interviewed who did not engage in long-term, monogamous relationships (Translation: He never had sex with anyone other than his wife and, quite separately, the woman he secretly kept) either engaged in a ménage à trois or were approached to try one.

"He liked to watch. He had been a drug addict and alcoholic for so many years that he couldn't get an erection," said Lillian, who was kept by an extremely wealthy and prominent actor whose work was seen internationally. "His thing was watching two women touch each other and himself.

"He led an extremely active fantasy life. He had floodlights and a circular bed and a special holder on the wall where he could attach a video camera if he wanted. He had a closet full of sexy clothing for women to wear and he managed to coerce some of the most successful women in Hollywood into coming to our little get-togethers.

"I still don't know how he did it with them. Some were coke whores, sure, and we always had a good supply. I mean, do you think I could stomach that bullshit if I wasn't stoned at the time? But some of them seemed perfectly normal in every way except that they'd come over for our threesomes.

"He'd choreograph what we did. I'm not kidding. He'd dress us as harem slaves or businesswomen or cops or whatever he fancied. Only once were we just naked at the start. We always had to be something else.

"Usually he watched, bringing us orally to orgasm. Sometimes he wanted to participate, constantly shifting who was touching whom.

"A few times he wanted to have us act out fantasies around him. He had us dress as cops in jackets, caps, badges, and gun belts but nothing else. We had to handcuff him to the bed, then read him his Miranda rights and tell him what a naughty boy he was. Then we'd spank him and suck him for what must have been an hour before he'd be satisfied.

"It was so weird I finally couldn't handle it, stoned or not. He said it was okay, that he understood my feelings. He just didn't make me do it anymore. Two girls would come around after that, not one, and I would go out with my friends."

"He had me raped," said Tanya. "He had this girl from the Philippines come in and told me she was going to have sex with me. I told him no way in hell, and then he wrestled me onto the bed. He held me there while she began licking my body and forcing herself between my legs. I fought him, but he was too strong. He seemed to get stronger as he got more excited.

"Eventually he entered me, hurting me because I didn't want him. Later he made me lick her between the legs. It was sickening.

"We had been together for six months when he took me to a room he had in his office. It was in a private area, like an apartment off where he worked where he could stay if he needed to work unusually late and didn't want to go home.

"He told me that he wanted to try something a little kinky. He had always been a little odd, but with what he was giving me, I always indulged him. I mean, it seemed like the least I could do. Anyway, it turned out he wanted to tie my hands together, then tie them overhead to a couple of hooks he had embedded in the wall. I didn't mind and it was obvious that this was not the first time he had used the room this way because why else would the hooks have been there?

"Anyway, once he got me so I was suspended, he opened my blouse, then took off my skirt, stockings, and panties so I was naked from the waist down. Then he pressed a button on one wall and another woman came out of the bedroom. She came over to me and began touching my body. She unhooked my bra, then worked it over my breasts enough so that she could suck my nipples.

"I was extremely uncomfortable and didn't know what to do. I told him that I didn't think this was such a good idea, but I don't think he was listening anymore. His face was flushed and I could see that even with his suit still on, he was getting an erection.

"Suddenly he just shouted, 'Enough!' and the woman backed off. She turned toward him, stripped naked, and held out her hands to be tied like mine. He also attached her to the hooks, then removed his jacket, loosened his tie, and went to a closet where he got out something . . . I don't know how to describe it . . . like a padded whip, I guess. He had us turn and face the wall while he spanked us with it, laughing, talking about what a good time we were all having.

"He didn't really hurt me. And he untied us a few minutes later so he could use a hideaway bed he had in the office for sex with me. He didn't want her participating, just watching. Then he wanted her to arouse him orally so he could have her as well while I watched.

"I really don't know what it was. A power thing, maybe? I know that I didn't want anything to do with him after that. It was all so strange the way he introduced it."

And finally there was Rena who was kept by a man who liked to sleep three in a bed. "He was totally faithful to me when he wasn't with his wife," she said. "But once a week he would bring a call girl to the place he bought me. There would be no sex involved. He would turn on some classical music on the stereo, have us all take showers, then get into bed together. I would be on his left, the call girl would be on his right, and we'd all just lie there, listening to music. Sometimes he'd have us drink champagne or smoke a joint. Then we'd just lie there until he fell asleep.

"I never asked him what it was all about. He never had sex with these girls. I don't know what it was all about."

Sex by the Numbers

"We become great technicians," said Sylvia, a woman who has been kept since her teenage years by a succession of men in Los Angeles, London, and elsewhere. "I thought I enjoyed sex when I was first kept. It seemed fun, but what did I know?

"Then I got in with men who had very definite wants. I had one U.S. senator I was with for two years who said that I gave the best head he'd ever had and that was why he kept me around.

"I liked that. I liked having a skill men admired. If you have a sense of self-worth, being called the best cocksucker a man's ever had seems like a real put-down. But nobody ever told me I was good at anything before, so I became a technician. The men loved it but it was sex by the numbers for me.

"Things got so bad that there was one man I was with for just a couple of weeks. I moved in with him and was going to be kept by him, but he made too many demands. In fact, by the time we were through, I realized that I had to get out of that life.

"It was just like that book *9½ Weeks* where a woman told of her sexual affair. I was at a low point in my life, so anything he wanted to do, I did. I was the housemaid, dusting the house, and he was the master who came upon me, was overwhelmed with lust, and had sex with me on the dining room table. I let him put a dog collar around my neck one Sunday morning when we were going to spend the morning in bed, reading the paper. He attached a leash to the collar, then every time he wanted sex, he'd yank on the leash and I'd rush over and either give him head or let him take me from behind.

"We did everything. One morning he had me go in the shower so he could be a burglar who 'surprised' me and screwed me under the water. He tied me spread-eagle one night, had sex with me, then wouldn't let me loose. He'd fall asleep, then awaken and do it again and again. When I told him I had to go to the bathroom, he gagged me and wouldn't free me until I thought I couldn't hold it anymore and was trying to scream at him to let me go.

"Whatever he wanted, I did. And if I had control, I wanted to be perfect for him. I wanted him to feel like every other woman he might screw would be a letdown.

"It didn't end until I took a good look at him. He was using me, sometimes hurting me, a real sleaze ball. There was no thought of my wants. He wanted me to tell him how much fun I was having doing the things he liked, but that wasn't true. Some of it might have been fun if he had been concerned with my pleasure, but he wasn't. He was acting out every fantasy he could think of and I was just a receptacle for his cock. I guess it was him, more than anyone, who shocked me into wanting to change."

The Best Sex Is No Sex

"Many of my kept friends are kept by old men who haven't gotten it up in years. They want the image of having a beautiful girl on their arms. They want people thinking that even though they are seventy-five years old, they're having sex five times a day like a young macho stud," said Elaine.

"These guys will pay any price for the image. They get a girl an apartment, buy her clothing, jewels, an expensive car. All they want is for her to be seen with them and no one else. They're paying her to keep their secret, to let them be the envy of their friends.

"They're not kidding anyone. You get a guy who's seventy-five and he's running around in a Jaguar with gold chains around his neck and some girl the age of his granddaughter fawning all over him . . . Who's being fooled? There's no way a girl like that is going to be going with an old man unless she's being paid to do it. And if she's being paid, he's probably impotent like most of them are.

"These are the guys who were messing around with everything because they had the money to try anything they wanted. Maybe they were great in bed when they were young. Maybe they just jerked off inside her and left every partner thinking that a vibrator would show more emotion. I don't know.

"What happens is that these guys drink too much, they do too many drugs, and pretty soon they can't get it up. Probably half the guys they party with have the same problem for the same reasons, but none of them have the guts to do anything about it. They get some girl who's willing to be kept and they pay her so well, she'll go along with anything. You want her to be subtle, implying an intense relationship that is too personal to share, she'll take that role. You want her fawning all over her lover, she'll take that role. She'll brag that he keeps her exhausted in bed if that's what makes him happy. What does she care? She's got what she wants and he's making no demands on her."

How to Become a
Kept Woman

S ome kept women are groomed for the position. Others fall into the life-style by chance. At the extremes are women like myself whose histories of physical or emotional child abuse, perceived abandonment, sexual violence and seduction all can lead to an adult whose thinking is disturbed.

The following case histories reveal women whose decisions to be kept were made consciously and repeatedly throughout the years. One woman has made being kept an ongoing life-style. Others tried the experience but once, then stayed with it as long as the man would have them.

We'll call her Marian McKenzie, a woman who is one of the most glamorous personalities in show business. She has appeared in films, on the pages of *Vogue* magazine, and now is part of an extremely popular television show. Her husbands, and there have been four of them, were all wealthy, yet she considers a "bad year" one in which she earns only three hundred thousand dollars. And for many years, Marian was a kept woman.

"We weren't poor as kids. There were five of us in the family and we lived in a rambling old house that was always painted, with a garden in back and the lawn well maintained. It was in a working-class area, but the kind of location where they used to say that the people were 'house-proud.'

"I never knew just what my father did for a living. He was a laborer at first. I remember him picking up his toolboxes and going off to work on construction jobs during the day. He also had a night job as a janitor in one of the big high rises in downtown Los Angeles. I was maybe four or five then and I can remember his taking me with him some nights. I was the oldest and Mama stayed home with the other kids. I didn't know why he took me. I just remember being fascinated by all the different offices, looking in people's desk drawers and studying the pictures they had on their walls. My father said that so long as I didn't move anything, I could look at anything I wanted.

"Then he had a store of some kind. I guess it was a little like a cross between a 7-Eleven and a general store. He sold food and pop and candy, but he had toys and hardware and I don't remember what else. I remember that there were always men playing cards in the back room and that some of them smoked those big, smelly cigars.

"Looking back, now, I think he probably ran a gambling place. It wouldn't have been uncommon back then, though the one good thing Mama always said about him was that he didn't play the horses like my uncle Salvatore. Uncle Sal always had a 'sure thing' and Uncle Sal's sure things always liked to lie down and take a nap to get the strength to finish the race. He was always broke and always hitting on my father for ten or twenty dollars. I guess my father must have taken a piece of the action, but I really don't know. When you're a kid you don't ask about things like that. Whatever's happening in your life you just take for granted.

"We may not have been poor but my mother was obsessed with money. She told me that she wanted me to have all the advantages she never had. She was the first generation over here, her parents came on the boat from Italy. They were poor people, cleaning houses, taking in boarders, doing whatever they had to do to get by.

"We lived near Hollywood and my mother got me lessons in dancing, acting, and modeling. The schools weren't very good, but they told us lies about their graduates and my mother believed them enough that she got me an agent and started sending me on cattle calls when I was sixteen."

A "cattle call" is the term used when a producer or director is casting one or more roles in a film or play and is willing to look at anyone who shows up. Officially these are known as "open auditions" or "open casting calls" to distinguish them from the ones where only specific actors or actresses are asked to try out. A cattle call is an audition where the producer advertises for "long legged blondes who can dance. Must look no older than twenty-five." Or "men and women under thirty with good bodies for possible parts in a film taking place in a health club." Dozens or hundreds of hopefuls will show up, some of whom actually look appropriate for the role being cast. Cattle calls are the most frustrating and least productive ways to find work, yet often the only opportunities for unknowns.

The cattle calls were not productive for Marian but the agent told her that she could meet influential men if she attended some of the parties they gave. He said that they were always delighted to have talented young actresses sitting around the pool in bikinis to add beauty to the surroundings.

"I believed him and my mother told me to go. She knew that what they really wanted was to have sex with a teenager and I was too naïve to realize that she was pimping me. She just told me to have fun and not worry about getting to school the next day. This was more impor-tant.

"The first party I went to was wonderful. The guy had one of those mansions in the Hollywood hills where they have marble floors, crystal chandeliers, and a pond filled with *koi* [large, colorful, extremely expensive Oriental carp] that had an underground connection into a similar pond inside the entranceway of the house. There were servants everywhere, passing out drinks and food, taking whatever you were drinking and keeping it replenished even before you could finish the last drops. I got quite drunk, sitting on the piano and doing my audition piece.

"I think if anyone had tried to take advantage of me, things might have been different. But everyone was enjoying this drunk kid with the big boobs and the skinny waist. They all knew I was underage and maybe that had something to do with the fact that they didn't hit on me right then. The closest someone came was a producer who handed me his card and suggested that my mother and I make an appointment to see him.

"A producer! God, what that word meant to me then. I knew I had been discovered. I was going to be in movies!

"The guy really was a producer, but he had made only two kinds of films in his life. One type was made and put on the shelf, never being shown anywhere. Those were the days when you could take a lot of tax write-offs. A lot of people put up money for movies that were filmed but never shown. Some of the biggest stars in Hollywood appeared in them, but they were never intended for release. You release them and, good or bad, one of them might have been successful, God forbid. The idea was to lose money because then you could pad your taxes somehow and take off more money than you actually put up for the picture. It's all too complicated for me, but even the major studios made movies for tax write-offs instead of the audience.

"The other movies he made were not very nice. These weren't porno flicks but tits-and-ass things for the drive-ins. *Blood Sucking Amazons from Venus* or *Island of the She Devil Warriors*. That kind of thing. There were a lot of girls with tits hanging out of their costumes and a couple of good-looking studs who had to conquer their man-hating queen. Or there would be some monster wearing what looked like a dime-store mask who would tear off your clothing while you went screaming down the hall, clutching your almost naked breasts. Real art stuff for the drive-in movie crowd.

"Being in any of those would have been all right with me, but that's not what he had in mind. He explained that he had to travel around the world on business and he needed a hostess to accompany him. He liked traveling with a beautiful, sophisticated, articulate young woman. He said that he had one he usually used, but she was busy making a film and he wondered if I would take her place for a few weeks at least.

"What he meant is that he and his girlfriend had had a fight over her banging the cameraman on the set of their last picture. He wanted to make her jealous by taking some big-boobed bimbo around the world with him and I was just what he needed. I think Mama understood all this, but she pretended it was a great business opportunity. She said I would get a far better education than I ever would in school, and since the producer was such a gentleman, she knew everything would be fine.

"I later learned that Mama got a thousand dollars from him for agreeing to the trip.

"We didn't have sex for three days, which with this guy was probably some sort of record. He kept everything straight with me until I complained that my back ached. We had flown to Paris where he actually did have something to do with the overseas distribution of his pictures. We had separate suites in the hotel, and I told him that I was going to take a long, hot shower to relax my muscles. I figured that I had sat wrong on the plane and I was nervous, so that didn't help, either.

"He suggested that he rub my back. He said a massage would do me more good and I could follow up with the shower when the muscles had relaxed.

"I was a virgin back then, but not because I wanted to be. Had I stayed in school, I was planning to work my way through the entire football squad, including the four-eyed, acne-covered runt who was the team manager. I was ready for any experience except rape and I might have gone for that if I could have chosen my attacker.

"The producer played it straight. He had me lie on the bed with all my clothes on. He worked my shoulders and neck, then gradually went down my back. He worked my legs as well, staying down near my ankles.

"At first he was quiet. Then, as I relaxed and gave myself up to the good feelings, he began talking about how pretty I was, what a great future I had ahead of me. I became flushed and didn't pay too much attention as he moved toward my genitals.

"The guy had great patter. He convinced me that I should unzip my dress and loosen my bra so that I would not feel constricted. I was still lying on my stomach, so I figured there was nothing wrong with it. Besides, I liked his touch and was beginning to get quite horny. When he finally worked his way to my thighs, I was ready for him.

"I don't remember too much after that. At some point I know he undressed. I also remember his putting his cock on my hand when my arms were by my side and he was still rubbing my back. I got scared for a moment, then began stroking it, hearing him gasp with pleasure. By the time he had me turn onto my back, we were both ready and there was almost no pain when he entered me. It was the most intense feeling I had ever known, probably because I had been wanting it for so long.

"Sex was just a natural part of the rest of that trip. He gave me his

American Express Card to buy clothing in all the stores. He probably expected me to go for designer gowns, but I bought all the funky stuff that was so popular back in the 1960s. We actually went to Carnaby Street when I was in London and I went crazy in all the boutiques. I thought I was spending a fortune, but my total purchases probably came to less than I would spend now on a 'big girl's' designer dress."

The time was the early 1960s, a period that was the end of the studio star system. There were still a few contract players at the studios, men and women who received a salary while taking lessons in acting, singing, and dancing. They were given parts in films and billed as "guest stars" on television programs. The studio publicity departments carefully nurtured their images, building their reputations in the press so that they became well known to the public and, hopefully, would develop into major box office attractions.

There were also the starlets, women not under contract but used as play toys among some of the producers, directors, and top actors. They often lived with the men, traveled with them, and were rewarded by bit parts in major films and starring roles in less-respected productions. Marian became a starlet, kept by first one producer, then another. Her mother was thrilled.

The agent Marian obtained proved as disreputable as her mother. Marian was a commodity to be sold to the highest bidder, a piece of meat to be shared among the less-reputable movers and shakers in the film industry. But she also was something more. She was a beautiful woman with what one art director called a "drop-dead face."

"I was lazy. I wanted money, fame, and power," said Marian, speaking of those early days. "I began doing modeling and was well paid for it. But I figured that if men would buy me jewels, take me on exotic trips, and treat me to luxury, that was a better way to go."

Marian had one insight that most kept women addicted to the life-style seem to lack. She was aware that life as she knew it might be temporary. She knew that traveling on a yacht was not the same as owning it. She made it clear to the men in her life that she delighted in jewelry and quickly learned to tell quality pieces. These she put in a safe-deposit box, her holdings worth well in excess of a million dollars by the time she was forty.

Marian's first marriage, at nineteen, was a brief one. Her agent introduced her to a well-placed talent manager who was capable of getting women in jobs their fame might otherwise not warrant. No one would say why he was owed so many favors, though it was rumored that he was bisexual and could blackmail some of the most powerful men in the industry. Whatever the case, the marriage lasted long enough for Marian to begin making movies and to develop a more extensive fashion modeling career in New York. Then, when she felt she had gone as far as she could go, she divorced him and had an affair with one of the most successful stars in Hollywood.

"The bastard used me without giving anything in return. I knew he was married to some rich bitch but I didn't know how much he liked his wife's money. I was another fuck for him. He said I'd have to be satisfied in bed because if he went out of his way to help my career, his wife would know he slept with me. He said I had no talent so I'd have to screw my way into a picture. He was a real son of a bitch."

Yet the truth was that Marian had almost no talent. She was of limited ability at best and refused to take acting lessons or other training that would help her improve. She was an excellent model, a beautiful woman, and has a gift of gab that has made her successful with talk shows. But as one critic not so kindly put it, "Her range of emotions runs from A to B." The line was not original with her, though it was appropriate.

"The one thing I learned was that if you're a woman, the only ability you need is between your legs. You fuck the right guy at the right time and he'll keep you in the manner to which no woman is accustomed."

Marian let herself be kept by a progression of men, carefully selecting her next target while her current affair was intense. Each had to be rich enough to buy her top-quality jewelry. Each had to give her presents— a Rolls-Royce, expensive clothing, an elaborate house. Yet she also found a way to show her disdain for the men. She kept the jewelry ("my 'social security,' " she jokes) but deliberately destroyed many of her other gifts. She refused to service the Rolls-Royce, telling her husband that she was faithfully having the oil changed, the engine tuned, and the other routine maintenance done, until she called him to say the engine had burned up on the highway. Furs were often "mislaid" in restaurants where she had lunch. Even her stepchild was consciously abused because he was husband number three's pride and joy.

The calculated actions had an underlying tone of self-hate, though. She disliked intercourse but delighted in sexual foreplay that was sadomasochistic in nature, with her taking the role of the victim. She frequently drank too much at parties, shocking friends who heard her coming on to men by saying, "Beat me and eat me. Beat me and eat me." She often got takers, slipping off to a bedroom, then returning a half hour later smiling and happy. A few times she was obviously bruised and the man she was with was known to also like violence, a fact that seemed to corroborate the idea that she was doing more than talking an odd sexual line.

"She used to want me to tie her up, then spank her until her cheeks were red," said her third husband, still dismayed by the request. "I hated it, but it turned her on."

"She told me to 'rim' her," said a producer with whom she lived for several months. "I had never heard the term before, though she said her first husband taught it to her. She wanted to have me lie on my back, then she would sit bare-assed so she was positioned just above my face. Then I was supposed to take my tongue and slowly lick around her anus until she came. Even clean out of the shower, I found the whole thing disgusting. I felt she couldn't have sex unless she was in a position that was humiliating for the man."

Marian is currently involved with her fourth husband, a major figure in the film industry. She began an affair with him while still married to her third husband, carrying on for more than two years before she divorced the one to marry the other.

"She told me to take good care of her honey," said the New York hair stylist who was cutting her third husband's hair at the time she introduced him to the man to whom she is currently married. "She said he was going to be her next husband. She said she liked the way I was styling her current husband's hair, and since both men were of a similar build and age, she thought I should do both. That was probably two years before her divorce."

It is interesting to note that her current husband also has a history of being unable to commit to a relationship. He was married and had a mistress in California at the time he began having an affair with Marian in New York. Just before his divorce from his previous wife, he convinced his mistress that she would be the person he would marry when he was free. The mistress was quite comfortable with the idea that he cheated on his wife but she was horrified to find that he also cheated on her.

In addition, the man had a reputation for maintaining an active casting couch. It was said in Hollywood that if a beautiful but unknown actress wanted to appear on certain television series where beautiful women frequently had minor speaking parts, all they had to do was have sex with him. He was later fired, allegedly for such practices.

For the moment, Marian has the kept woman's dream. Her husband is rich, powerful, and unquestioning about the jewelry he buys her which she seems seldom to wear. She has a top-rated television program, a steady income, and has retained her beautiful face so unlined that she can still model fashions meant for much younger women. Yet if she is running true to her past, she is also working to find the next man to take care of her.

Annie Harrelson was a singer whose skills enabled her to perform on Broadway as well as in the major nightclubs in New York. She was beautiful, talented, and adored from afar by Jack Peters, an extremely wealthy man with vast interests in sports. He owned winning race horses, athletic teams, and other ventures that enabled him to maintain several houses, yachts, and a standard of living that was impressive even for the rich. He also had great power and influence, his wealth being large enough for him to be able to finance theatrical productions and/or films if he so chose.

Jack was uncertain how to meet Annie, though he regularly attended any shows where she performed. Finally he hired a man to approach her, a man who would discuss the multimillionaire's desire to meet her. He had the man explain that Jack could have a very powerful influence on her career and she would do well to meet him. In fact, if she played her cards right, Jack might back a musical in which she would star.

Annie began to date the man. She was single and he was married, yet the two became quite close.

Eventually they decided to have a life together. He bought her an apartment on Park Avenue and a second house in Beverly Hills. In that way she could work on either coast and have a place where they could be together.

Annie was used to being somewhat of a gypsy because her profession forced her to be on the road rather frequently. She realized that if she was married, she would continue her career and probably be unable to see her husband any more frequently than she and Jack were together. She knew that she loved him and did not want to end a relationship that gave her everything she desired. Thus they stayed together until he died—twenty-seven years later.

The reading of the will proved most interesting. He was determined that she would want for nothing the rest of her life, yet he also did not wish to hurt his wife. She had suspected that he had a woman on the side, though she could never prove it. Even after his death he had protected her from knowing, leaving great sums of money to the woman he kept, though arranging for it to pass through one of his companies in monthly payments. It appeared that she was simply a large business debt being repaid in installments. The wife never had to endure the pain of knowing the full truth and the woman he kept was assured of a life of luxury whether or not she ever worked again.

Evelyn was twenty-three years of age and a former *Playboy* magazine cover model. She was working at the Playboy Club in New York where she met Bill, a handsome man in his sixties, who asked her to dinner and bought her an expensive diamond. He took her to expensive restaurants, bought her costly gifts, and then, in just a few weeks, told her that he would like to keep her. He said that he was in and out of town on an irregular basis. He might be in town once or twice a month. He might be in town a little more often. He would buy her a condominium that would be hers even if he left her. However, if she left him, the condominium would he his.

Evelyn went to see her therapist to discuss the offer. The therapist explained the potential emotional pitfalls of such a relationship but she decided that they would be worth it for her.

The arrangement delighted Evelyn at first. She received fur coats and luxury gifts. When he traveled, he would send her to cities such as Monte Carlo, then meet her there so that the relationship would not be discovered. He also maintained a private jet which occasionally took her to wherever he was located. In addition she received a salary of five thousand dollars a month beyond the money she needed for living expenses.

Bill had only one restriction. He told her that she could do anything she wanted away from the condominium but she had to be available to him whenever he called. At no time was she to have an affair in the apartment he had purchased, though he would be understanding if she had men on the side.

The arrangement lasted for five years. Then Evelyn met an actor and fell in love with him. She told him what she did and how she made her money, a situation that seemed to please him. However, as time passed, he realized that the situation was upsetting for him. He became jealous and possessive, asking her to give up Bill.

Evelyn went to Bill during his next visit to California, telling him that she had to leave their relationship. She was not in love with him and could not continue as they had been.

Bill agreed to the split, reminding her of their arrangement. He ordered her out of the apartment, allowing her to take her clothing and whatever money she had set aside from her savings, but nothing else.

Evelyn was determined to make her relationship with the actor successful. She found a job and began working, living with the actor. However, the actor continued to be irrationally jealous. He kept talking about Bill and the way Evelyn had allowed herself to be used before she left him. It was talk she could not handle, so she ended the relationship.

Evelyn returned to Bill to ask to go back to their old relationship. Bill, who had professed to love her, told her that what she desired was impossible. He had replaced her with another woman.

Mark was an extremely wealthy hotel owner with property in New Jersey, Nevada, and elsewhere. He was a principal in casinos and an extremely powerful man. He had also been married forty-two years and had two children.

One day Mark met Anna, a young attorney who fascinated him. He pursued her, finally convincing her to date him. They liked each other and eventually became sexually involved with each other.

Gradually a pattern developed in the relationship. They would be together every week, and when he had to travel abroad, he began taking her with him.

For two and a half years they carried on their affair until Anna realized that she could not handle the emotional stress. She wanted him to be free to marry her or she wanted to end the relationship. Loving him but not being able to have him all the time was too difficult, so she gave him an ultimatum. He was to either leave his wife or Anna would leave him.

Mark was extremely blunt with Anna. He said that he would not leave his wife because he could not afford to do so. His work required that he have personal access to many millions of dollars at any given time. His property and personal holdings regularly had to serve as collateral for the business deals in which he was engaged. Since his residence was in a community-property state, he could not get a divorce without cutting his wealth in half. Although this would still leave him a very rich man, it would leave him with too few assets to continue on the business scale where he wished to operate. As a result, he intended to stay married, much as he loved Anna.

Anna understood the business side of Mark's work and realized that what he said was true. She knew that his business was important to him and he could not give up his work for the marriage to her. Instead, he offered her a compromise.

Mark agreed to treat Anna as his wife. She could legally take his name. He would arrange for a place where she could live. He would establish an expense account for her. And he guaranteed that he would spend at least three days a week and half of the holidays with her. He said that she could adopt a child if she wanted. She could give up her work as an attorney. Whatever she wanted that would normally be possible in a marriage she would have.

Anna liked the idea. Together they drew up a contract outlining the arrangements they would share. Among the terms was an annual pay arrangement that provided her with an extremely high income. In addition, if either one of them ended the relationship, she would receive severance pay equal to one year's pay for each year they had been together. The money would be put into a trust fund for her each year so there would be no chance of his cheating.

Anna enjoyed the life-style at first. She determined the cost of the arrangement to him and realized that he probably spent approximately $250,000 per year to keep her. This large amount of money, including expensive presents, excited her. She delighted in the idea of a man being so taken by her that he would spend so much money.

For seven years they shared this life-style. For Christmas she received a new Mercedes convertible. For her birthday, she received a trip around the world. Luxuries became routine.

As so often happens in these circumstances, there came a time when Anna fell in love with a man, ending her relationship with Mark. What she did not expect was for him to fall apart. He begged her to return, unable to handle the separation. He even went so far as to threaten to kill them both, a threat that she took seriously because he was known to have had a violent past.

Today they are still together. She is forty-four; he is seventy-three. At first the renewed relationship was one of dominance and fear. But gradually Anna accepted the reality that she would be staying with Mark for the rest of his life. She was adored. She was kept in fabulous style. And she would still be relatively young when he died, enabling her to experience other relationships as a wealthy woman in a few years.

Ramón, fifty-five, was an extremely wealthy Mexican. He was one of the fortunate men in his country, a nation that seems divided between the very rich and the very poor. His family had been worth millions of dollars for the past three generations. They influenced the nation's politics and were considered among the most important families in the country.

Ramón knew only the best. He traveled the world, maintained polo ponies, threw elaborate cocktail parties for hundreds of guests at a time, and owned thousands of acres of land surrounding his several houses. His lettuce crops alone required six thousand workers to pick and process.

It was in Las Vegas that Ramón met Norma. She was an actress who, in the past, had dated or been kept by extremely wealthy, powerful men in show business. One was an actor whose family had strong political connections. Another was British, honored by the Queen and extremely wealthy. And a third was a top entertainer appearing in the highest-priced clubs, performing on television, and earning several million dollars a year. It was the entertainer who had most recently kept her.

Norma had obtained a job acting as a hostess for a Las Vegas convention that Ramón and other rich landowners were attending. She was a gorgeous blue-eyed blonde, six feet tall, with a perfect figure. He saw her, then walked over to her and said, "You know, you're something that I've always dreamed of but never thought I'd ever see. Your white skin, your blue eyes, your beautiful natural blond hair . . . I would like just to be your friend. You fascinate me so much."

Because she was a hostess, Norma had to be nice to him. However, she was uncertain what to think as he explained that he was a married man with five children who wanted her to come to Mexico and be his guest at his villa. "I'll send you a plane ticket. Just come, have dinner with my family and me."

Ramón's words did not seem like a proposition. He was intriguing and she decided to go to his house, seeing no reason why there might be a problem.

That night, after a party for the people attending the convention, he suddenly appeared, walking over to her with an envelope. He told her that it contained a little tip to thank her for her graciousness as a hostess. Inside, she discovered, was ten thousand dollars in hundred-dollar bills.

Three months passed without her hearing from him again. However, she talked constantly about him to her friends. She said that she would love to marry a man like that. It was too bad he was already married with children. He was nice, generous, and obviously taken with her. Norma had become Cinderella, only this time she was waiting for Prince Charming.

As is typical with many kept women and the men with whom they are involved, Norma really did not know Ramón. He was drawn to her physical beauty and her professional charm. She saw a nice man who did not try to get her into bed. He was also obviously rich and quite generous. For them to pursue each other was to pursue a fantasy. He did not want to know what she was like with her makeup gone, her morning breath, her voice harsh from stress she might be undergoing, when she was tired. She did not want to know whether he might be abusive in bed, a workaholic who placed women in luxury then never saw them for days or weeks at a time, or anything else that might challenge the fantasy.

Another week passed, then she received a package containing several thousand dollars and a round-trip ticket to the Mexican state where he lived. The money was to be used to buy clothing before visiting his villa.

Upon arrival, Norma was overwhelmed by the experience of his wealth. It wasn't just the opulent surroundings, though the possessions were obviously worth millions. What amazed her was the style with which he lived.

"I was assigned a personal maid and butler for my waking hours. No matter where I went, no matter what I did, one of them was always there to anticipate my wants. If I had a drink, a fresh one would be waiting the moment I finished the first. If I wanted a snack at midnight, an opulent array of foods would be spread before me to sample. It was like something you might imagine on the wealthy Southern plantations when they still had slaves doing all the work."

Norma had a wonderful time in Mexico. She met Ramón's wife and children, was treated like royalty, and spent four days delighting in luxury. He made no effort to do anything more than be friendly.

After Norma returned home to Los Angeles, she received a telephone call from Ramón. He was coming to the city on business with a couple of associates. He wondered if she could find a couple of friends so that they could all go out to eat. She agreed and they again had a good time. They went to the most expensive places in town and he made no effort to do anything more than be her friend.

A week later she received another telephone call from Ramón. He had to go to Monte Carlo to do some gambling. He offered to take her with him, arranging to pick her up at the airport in his private plane, paying her for her time. She would act as his hostess, much as she had been a hostess in Las Vegas. Her pay would be five hundred dollars per day plus all expenses.

It was in Monte Carlo that Ramón got Norma into the bedroom and it was there that she found she was serious about him. The romance developed and he said that he wanted to keep her.

Norma was concerned with the fact that Ramón was married. However, he explained that Mexican men from his background were married because marriage was necessary for their social position in life. "When I am in the United States, I am single," he explained.

Norma objected at first, but Ramón was persistent. He flooded her with gifts and the intimacy they shared was mutually enjoyed. Finally she agreed to the arrangement. She went on the payroll of one of his companies, receiving five thousand dollars per week in cash and a luxury condominium in Century City, California. This happened in 1973 and the arrangement continues to this day.

Ramón and Norma are together once or twice a week. They eat in the finest restaurants. They are seen throughout Los Angeles and it is assumed that they are married.

The couple also travel together, going throughout the world, except to Mexico. It is the only country where Norma cannot go. It is also the only country where Ramón's wife is allowed to travel.

Eleanore never intended to become a kept woman. She was quiet, almost shy, a highly skilled executive secretary who enjoyed walks in the woods, reading novels, and listening to music. She wanted to marry, to be close to a man, and she frequently dated both within the company and people she met through handling business matters for her boss.

As is typical for most all of us, Eleanore was drawn to her opposite. The men she dated were aggressively outgoing. They liked team sports, nightclubs, and large parties. Eleanore was uneasy in such circumstances, yet she wanted to be more outgoing and enjoyed being encouraged to participate by the men she dated.

Invariably the issue of sex arose after a few dates. Eleanore had no strong feelings one way or another about sex, and she thought it could be an enjoyable part of an intense relationship. She saw no reason why she should wait for marriage and, though she was not promiscuous, she found that she enjoyed the idea of gentle lovemaking with a man she liked. However, her reality was quite different.

"They didn't care about my needs," she commented later. "All they thought about was their own pleasure. If they got it up, then obviously I was ready for them. And when they were finished, I had to be satisfied because they were. Most of them thought that a good night of sex was getting it off four or five times in an hour or two. They couldn't understand that I wanted them to slow down, to touch my body, not just grab my breasts and genitals before entering. I wanted tenderness and they wanted to see how many times they could jerk off inside me.

"I had a friend who used to jokingly call her periods of celibacy between sex partners the time when she was 'dating Mr. Hand.' I got to feeling that as much as I wanted a man, if the only sex I was going to have was with men who never thought about anyone other than themselves, I might as well masturbate. At least I could control the pacing."

Eleanore came to the conclusion that she would probably never marry. She didn't want to be without a man in her life, but she also was tired of being bullied in relationships. The men in her past were unthinking, uncaring, self-centered individuals who failed to realize just how they were acting. She accepted loneliness as a part of her future, then came to treasure the time she had to herself. She was not a recluse. She had friends. But the intimacy that can come between a man and a woman was something she accepted would never be enjoyed.

Several weeks after Eleanore made her decision, her boss, an older man whom she greatly respected, suggested that they work unusually late, taking a break for dinner in an expensive restaurant. He had to travel to Europe concerning a new account and needed to do extensive paperwork prior to the trip. He required her assistance and, though she would be paid well for the overtime, he felt guilty. He thought that the dinner would be a nice break and a small bonus for her hard work, even though he knew that she had no responsibilities waiting for her at home.

The dinner was more than a nice break. They talked about the office, her insights being unusually astute in his mind. He talked about books, the two of them discovering that they had similar tastes. And though in many ways he was similar to men she had dated in the past, he was older, more willing to listen, concerned with her feelings and not just his own.

The boss began taking Eleanore out with frequency after he returned from his business trip. No longer was their relationship one that related to business. They were friends and, after several weeks, lovers.

For the first time Eleanore knew sexual pleasure. Her boss was willing to take the trouble to ease her into intercourse, prolonging the foreplay and building the feelings. She began looking forward to sex, becoming aroused when they worked together.

It was two or three months after they first were intimate that Eleanore's boss suggested that she might want to move into a bigger apartment. He would be happy to underwrite the cost since they were spending so much time together and he knew she could not afford much more than she had. He also bought her more glamorous dresses for when they went out and, when she had car trouble, he bought her a new Cadillac, running the charge through the company.

"We were together three or four times a week which gave me plenty of time to myself. There were no pressures, and because we worked together, we always had plenty to talk about. I didn't care about the fact that he was married. If anything, it took pressure off me. I could have nice things, enjoyable sex, and a better apartment than I ever would have rented on my own and I didn't have to deal with the stress of having someone around me twenty-four hours a day.

"It's not easy living with someone else, you know. You give up a lot of yourself. There are times I want to let myself go, dressing like a slob and wandering around the apartment doing whatever I want to do. If my breath is bad from nibbling garlic-spiced foods or my hair needs washing, there's nobody around to complain. Married, I'd have to think about his feelings and behave in a way he'd want. This way I had the space to live my own life my own way, and because of that, I looked forward to pleasing him on those days when we were together. I know I was being kept, but so what? Who was getting hurt?"

The relationship lasted three years, until Eleanore was offered a better position by another company. "I wasn't looking for another job. I was just approached by the head of a company with whom we did business. He had worked with me on projects where I had to handle the day-to-day details for my boss and he liked what I did. There was a change in staffing at his place and he offered me a position with his company at a fifteen-thousand-dollar a year raise plus better benefits. I took it without question."

Eleanore did not think about how the new job would affect her being kept by her now ex-boss. However, they both quickly realized that what had been convenient and fun was becoming a chore. There was also a stress when they were together because they no longer felt that they could talk together about work they had once shared. Within six weeks, the affair was over. A few weeks after that, Eleanore began dating her boss in the new business. Shortly the previous pattern was repeated.

The paths to becoming a kept woman are many. Most of the women are beautiful, though in researching this book we found women who were grossly overweight, with features that were extremely unattractive, or in some other way counter to the logical view of what a kept woman should look like.

Some of the women worked for smaller companies in conservative regions where the idea of being kept would be shocking to anyone who might discover the truth. Others were already in glamour careers when the opportunity presented itself. A few were actually the aggressors, determined to enter the life-style with any man who would have them.

Yet they all came to share the sense of shallowness, of pain, of recognizing that no matter how they justified their existence, there was an underlying fear of commitment both on their parts and the part of the men who kept them.

"We were at this party in Beverly Hills," said Anna-Leigh. "A friend of mine was dating the lead singer of a rock group that was just beginning to become well known. There had been some stories on them in some of the celebrity magazines and it was rumored that *People* was going to do a major piece on them. They had been asked to come to the house of a famous entertainer for an affair he was having and my friend arranged for me to tag along.

"The party wasn't anything like I expected, though I don't know what I thought I'd find. I was feeling wild and had purchased some skintight leather slacks and a silk blouse you could see through when the light was right, and my hair was cut short on one side, long on the other, and then layered in what came close to being today's more conservative version of a punk hairstyle. I was wearing a twenty-dollar gold piece that had been made into a necklace and my watch was a Coram my parents had given me on my twenty-first birthday.

"At the time I was modeling, going to cattle calls at the studios, and taking lessons in acting, singing, dancing, and martial arts to help my career. My figure was tight and flawless, and the outfit I wore was meant to make me the center of attention.

"I'll call him Harry. He was the head of one of the studios, but he looked and moved like a star. He must have been fifty years old then and I was barely in my twenties. He brought me a glass of champagne, then began talking. He asked me about the necklace, then started talking about the career of Augustus Saint-Gaudens who had designed the coin I was wearing. He was an expert in medallic art and I was fascinated by the discussion.

"Things were getting a little out of hand at the party. There was unlimited booze and more types of drugs being done than I had ever seen before. People were slipping each other pills or going into the bathrooms to do lines of coke. The music kept getting louder and the guests raunchier.

"He suggested we get out of there and go to a restaurant he knew where we could get some good food and keep talking all night if we wanted. I agreed and we left, heading for the airport.

"Harry made a couple of calls on his car telephone as we drove toward the airport. I was feeling the effects of the alcohol, dozing in the car, and paid no attention to what he was doing until we actually pulled into one of the parking decks at LAX. 'We're not going to eat here?' I said. I mean, airports have never been known for their gourmet dining.

" 'We're still going to that restaurant I mentioned,' he said. 'It's in Las Vegas.'

"I didn't know what to say. There was a private jet fueled and ready with a pilot. A limousine was waiting at the airport when we arrived and we did go to that restaurant. Then we spent what was left of the night in a suite in Caesars Palace. The next day he gave me a thousand dollars to gamble with, then flew me back home.

"I was overwhelmed. Here I am, twenty-two years old, working in a profession that eats you alive at best, not really getting anywhere, when the head of a studio comes on to me like that. Then he tells me he's got to go to Rome that weekend because he's scouting for locations for a film his company's producing and I figure I'm getting the brush-off. I had spent the night with him, we had had sex, and I thought he was just a guy looking for a good time who felt that he had paid for it. Then he said, 'Why don't you come with me? I'll be gone a couple of weeks and I don't want to be apart from you that long.'

"I was speechless which, for me, is something like a miracle. I mean, I never shut up and I didn't know what to say. I even felt guilty for holding back a couple of hundred dollars from the money he gave me for gambling because I figured I should have something longer-term for what we had done.

"We were together for a year and I thought it was very intense. We went to New York together, Toronto, London, Paris . . . He consulted me on business deals. He asked me to read scripts the studio was considering because he valued my opinion. A couple of times he even had me take meetings with the writers for a show in development because he felt my ideas were stronger than theirs.

"I lived with Harry for a while, then he arranged for me to have a place of my own in Manhattan because he was spending so much time in the East and thought it would be better. What I didn't realize was that he was easing me out of his life. He had a new girl in Los Angeles, younger than I but the same type. He later said he was making the transition gradually as he wasn't sure she would work out."

For Anna-Leigh, the seduction began with the jet set life-style and was completed when she discovered that Harry respected her abilities. He eventually arranged for her to work in production in one of the networks in Manhattan, a job contact she gained through his influence but one she has kept for the last ten years because of her abilities.

For Marilyn, being kept meant staying in Cleveland, Ohio, where she was with some of the most powerful people in the city. "You have to understand where I was coming from. We were all kids raised in the Jewish ghettos on Kinsman and the Hundred and Fifth Street areas. The Kinsman Jews were the laborers in my day. They often lived in two-family houses, working blue-collar jobs. Sometimes the women stayed home with the children. Sometimes the women had to work. But either way there never was much money.

"The Hundred and Fifth Street area was better. There were Jewish lawyers, doctors, business owners. Most of the houses were single-family houses.

"I was raised on Kinsman but I dated some of the boys from the Hundred and Fifth Street area. They had cars and money to take you someplace nice. I always thought that what I wanted from life was to go to the fancy parties, the nice places to eat, the symphony."

Marilyn had a brief, "disastrous" marriage, then began working in the construction business. She was a bookkeeper, handled ordering, and gradually trained herself in other phases of the field. This brought her into contact with a number of developers at a time when Cleveland was becoming a center for growth. Millions of dollars were being made by even smaller companies and she was meeting with the major business leaders in the field.

"We would have business meetings into the evening and I thought I was just one of the boys," Marilyn recalls. "Then I was asked to go to one of the trade shows with a wealthy developer, and I still thought it was all business. He was extremely prominent, married, and had children. He did not have a reputation for playing around and he did not make a pass at me.

Soon Marilyn was traveling with the developer to Chicago, New York, and Detroit. It was in Detroit, over dinner at an expensive restaurant, that he made his offer.

"I'll call him Ben, though that wasn't his real first name. He told me that he admired me. He said that I had brains. The courage to live alone, and the guts to make a career in a man's business. He said that he wanted to see more of me, to do things for me.

"What he offered was a business proposition. He would buy me a large house in a good neighborhood. The house would be in my name and I could eventually sell it if I ever wanted to. He would buy me clothing, a new car every couple of years, take me to expensive restaurants, nice concerts, traveling when he could. I would lead my own life, being available to him whenever he called.

"There would be no marriage, no chance of marriage. His wife was his entree in the business world. She had the right connections with power brokers, money people, and the others he needed. He would not leave her because he was afraid he would also lose his business.

"I was safe. He wasn't in love with me and I wasn't in love with him. He was exciting in bed because he so thoroughly wanted me. I was his escape from the burdens he carried, yet there were no emotions involved. I knew he would not leave his wife and I knew that I might marry someone else some day. This way I had everything I wanted and so did he. We were using each other, and I suspect that each of us thought we were getting the better deal."

Annie is being kept by her ex-husband, a very successful doctor who lives from Monday through Friday with his twenty-two-year-old girlfriend. He pays the fifteen hundred dollar a month rent for her apartment. She drives a new Mercedes. She has periodic sex with her ex-husband and they often travel together. Yet despite the arrangement, she claims to hate the man, looking upon the money he spends on her as her "due."

Annie's background was one of violence and abuse. For eight years during her childhood, her uncle had sex with her, buying her silence with gifts of dolls she had wanted. The rapes were their "special secret," with no one realizing what was happening until her mother caught her burying the dolls in the backyard. The repeated burials seemed so unusual that her mother began probing the reasons, discovering for the first time what had been happening with the uncle.

Annie's parents reported the uncle to the authorities, prosecuting him and sending him to jail. But they did not bother getting professional help for Annie, deciding that she was young, resilient, capable of "bouncing back" from the nightmare. They were certain she would outgrow any problems. They were also certain that the family had suffered enough. There was no sense in bringing in strangers to hear Annie's story, even if those strangers were professionals trained to help abused children. As a result, Annie reached adulthood with great confusion over normal sexuality.

"All I wanted to do was escape from Orange County where I was raised," said Annie, explaining why she married Hank, an abusive man who was training to be a doctor.

Hank seemed to see Annie as a convenience. He was working endless hours at the hospital, never having time for a normal relationship. Being married was a convenience for the interns and residents who knew that their wives would always be available for sex whenever they had time off. Trying to date was almost impossible since their schedules had to remain flexible enough to allow for last minute cancellations. Thus a marriage seemed the ideal way to assure available sex.

The violence Annie experienced during her marriage was different from that which she had received at home. Some was physical. Some was verbal. Yet at least it was honest, open, up-front. There were no more dirty little secrets, though Annie remained haunted by her uncle's actions and the fear that somehow she had been a factor in causing the rapes.

The abuse continued in Annie's marriage. She had no interest in sex, yet learned to become skilled at bringing her husband to orgasm. She saw her control of his body as a way to dominate the relationship, the only positive action she felt she could achieve.

Eventually the abuse became overwhelming. Her husband brought home drugs, insisted that she take them, then had her overdose. Her heart was damaged and she came close to death when she realized that she could not continue in the marriage. She divorced him, broken in body and spirit.

Time passed and Annie grew increasingly angry toward her ex-husband. He moved in with a young girl, made an extremely large income, and continued to want to have sex with his ex-wife. Finally she decided to work out a business deal in which he would keep her.

The arrangement was a simple one. Annie's rent would be paid, she would receive the car, an allowance, clothing, and other necessities. She could work or not as she chose, date if she wished, all with no strings. She spoke of the agreement as someone might a pension plan. She had put in her time with her husband and this was the payback for her years of service.

Annie's ex-husband was also not bound by any constraints. He took a girlfriend who moved in with him, sharing his home and his bed during the week. On weekends he would travel to a ranch he owned where, on a frequent basis, he would be joined by Annie. The relationship would be a combination of conversation and sex, her performing as she always had, his being the fantasy life of a man who knows that there are two women "desirous" of his body. The fact that both women were actually using him was never expressed.

It was Arlen who made Annie realize she had a problem. Arlen is an actor, a man who proudly relates the fact that he works steadily in show business, an unusual situation for most members of the profession. Although Arlen is not his real name, his face is undoubtedly familiar from his minor roles in daytime soap operas, appearances in various television series, and occasional lesser roles in feature films. His income averages a thousand dollars a week from new performances and that is often supplemented by residuals and occasional television commercials. Thus he is quite comfortable by the standards of almost every community in the United States, except Beverly Hills.

Arlen is intelligent, good-looking, and aggressive. He has learned to accept the petty jealousies that are a part of his profession. He also has more interests than just what roles he might obtain. There is a sophistication about him that makes him seemingly special in a city filled with cutthroat neurotics desperate for the next deal and terrified of the first wrinkle to appear on their faces. And these attributes are ones that Annie noticed almost immediately.

Annie began dating Arlen, having met him at a party they both attended during the week. She liked him immediately and he was genuinely interested in her, not just in himself. "There's nothing special about me," he told her. "I make my living pretending to be someone else. It seems rather juvenile if you ask me, but I make more money than I could doing something in the real world, so I see no reason to stop."

The trouble was that Arlen's money was quite limited compared with the funds Annie was receiving from her ex-husband. He lived in a small, two-bedroom apartment that was comfortably furnished but in the "wrong" part of Los Angeles. His car was a Volkswagen GTI, quick enough to maneuver the freeways, easy to handle, with good gas mileage. It was part fun, part practical, and it was a joke to those who liked to be seen in a Rolls, an Excalibur, or some other vehicle that cost more than average Americans spent on their houses. But Arlen was not impressed with cars. He did not criticize Annie's Mercedes, but he also saw no practical reason to own one with the kind of in-town driving she did.

Even Arlen's clothing was "sensible." He bought his suits at a discount store, comfortable with the fact that he fit perfectly into off-the-rack styles in a city where a custom tailor was sometimes considered as much a necessity as a pool man, a maid, and a driver.

Seemingly against her will, Annie fell in love with Arlen. He did not beat her during sex, his tastes varied enough to maintain the excitement she craved, and he was gentle, loving, constantly concerned with her pleasure. He was proud to take her out, but his tastes tended to mid-priced restaurants and presents that were meaningful rather than carrying a large price tag. He confessed to having shopped in the Rodeo Drive area, the "in" place to shop for the extremely rich, only once, and then he had only gone to a bookstore which had since been closed. In short, he represented everything Annie could imagine as being good, dedicated, warm, caring, and decent.

There were other changes in Annie's life. First, she began enjoying sex. She had become a technician with her ex-husband, willing her body to not be stiff when she was touched. She had always hated intercourse but considered the time she spent in bed to be the payback for the items she received while being kept. Since she had to perform only on weekends, and not all weekends at that, the price seemed realistic. But with Arlen there was no tension. She relaxed at his touch, felt inner stirrings as he gently caressed her, was eager for him to enter her after long, slow, gentle foreplay. She achieved both orgasm and extreme pleasure from sex for the first time in her life.

Arlen was sent on location in Canada, a separation Annie thought she might enjoy. She had always been thrilled when her husband had left town for a few days during the period they were married. She reveled in the relative emptiness of their home, the quiet that came during his absence. But with Arlen, her feelings changed. She longed for his return, felt trapped in what had become unfriendly surroundings, avoided the bedroom as much as possible because he would not be there. For the first time in her life she understood what it was to love, to truly care about another human being. Even though they talked by telephone each night of the separation, she finally could stand it no longer and flew to where he was working, hanging around the set to be with him those few moments he was free.

When Annie and Arlen returned from the city where he had been working, he asked her to marry him. The proposal came as a surprise to her, though it was the only logical step in their relationship. All their friends thought that they would be perfect together. Everyone who had known Annie's past felt that the marriage would be a healing experience. But Annie said no.

"I can't give up my life-style," Annie explained. "There is no way I could marry Arlen and still fuck my husband on weekends. I feel guilty as it is, but what I'm doing isn't really so terrible. I mean, think of all the girls who have to occasionally go to bed with their bosses in order to keep their jobs. It's like I was in that kind of business, and we were married for years. It's not like he's some stranger. He had my body long before I knew Arlen, so there's nothing terribly dirty about it, is there?

"But I couldn't do that if I was married. I don't even know if he'd keep paying my rent and all because he's really a bastard. Always thinking of himself. He probably wouldn't feel obligated to keep paying me what I earned by being married to him if I was married to Arlen.

"And that's the trouble. Arlen doesn't make much money. Probably never will. Sure, we could get along okay in some other city. Move to Cleveland, maybe. Get a little house with a picket fence. Do the whole Suzie Housewife number.

"But Arlen can't work in Cleveland. He's an actor and a good one. He's always working but he's probably never going to be one of those lucky ones who becomes a star. I make more being single than I'd have if I was married. Maybe if I got a job to supplement what Arlen makes, but who'd want me? I'm past forty, no real skills other than getting my husband off in bed . . . I mean who'd want me?

"And I love Arlen. God, do I love Arlen. He's the most decent man I've ever known. No. He's more than that. Just not trying to use me would make him special in that way. Arlen can't use anybody. He's just loving, caring . . . He loves me. Can you imagine that? He actually loves me.

"I don't know if he's a complete fool or what. I mean, I keep thinking that if he knew what I was really like . . . And then I think that maybe he does and yet he still sticks around. It's all so scary . . ."

Annie remains in the two relationships, in love for the first time in her life yet unwilling to break her addiction to the kept life-style. Arlen seems to have accepted her decision and continues the relationship, though Annie wonders how long he'll tolerate the situation. She is frightened of losing him, though she also chooses to stay in the seemingly destructive pattern she has followed.

The Kept Woman Goes Professional

The stories of the kept women of the rich, famous, and powerful are primarily the stories of early childhood abuse, neglect, and/or abandonment, about longing for love, the seduction of money, and sexual manipulation. Often there is self-hate or a feeling of unworthiness in the women. And in some of them there is the feeling that they must appear to be perfect, top achievers in everything they do so no one will come to realize just how incompetent or unworthy they might really be.

In Chapter 1 an observer of the Hollywood scene cynically said, "It's the pussy business." She talked of women who marry the highest bidder being no different from those who choose to be kept. While the psychologists we interviewed strongly disagree with her interpretations of underlying motives, there are some kept women who become kept through professional training. They are sold to the highest bidder, a fact that makes them uncomfortable only when they have to return to the "dealer" after a relationship ends. And the women who broker the arrangements are world-class madams whose discretion and skill place them in positions of influence such that they are almost never in the public eye.

There are numerous differences between prostitutes and kept women as we have shown earlier. But one type of kept woman begins her career selling herself for money on a scale as far removed from the familiar street-corner prostitute as a head of state is different from the president of a local high school.

Of the several madams "selling" kept women in different parts of the United States, some agreed to be interviewed, though none would agree to have her name used. Others we learned about only through women who have worked for them in recent years. The stories were all surprisingly similar, with the main variation being the standards they maintained for their women.

Madam Charlotte: There is an elegance to Charlotte that is instantly visible despite the fact that she admits to being seventy and may be older. Her gait is rapid, her clothing impeccably tailored; she is the type of woman who frequently wears a hat and gloves to expensive restaurants. She dresses with the romantic grace of a bygone era, yet instead of looking dated, she appears to be setting the fashion trend that all other women will soon be following. There are obvious telltales of age, such as the glasses that were not needed until a couple of years ago, the use of taxis when she travels instead of the Mercedes she used to drive, the shoes that have lower heels and greater support than in the past. But these are minor. Charlotte appears to have been born into royalty, her presence receiving the respect that is earned, not demanded.

There are countless stories concerning how Charlotte first became a prostitute. There is talk of a bad marriage, an abusive childhood, the need to pay some horrendous family debt that could not be eliminated by any other means available to her. There is also talk that she simply enjoyed sex and that being paid for it allowed her to know the experience with greater frequency. The truth may die with her. All that is certain is that she was a stunning woman from the start, an elegant escort with the type of figure that could provoke lust in even the most staid of men.

The money Charlotte made during those early years was substantial. Her clients were wealthy and influential men who used her both as an escort and for sex. She was regularly seen at various state dinners throughout the world, attended the ballet and the symphony, always in a box seat, and dined in expensive restaurants. People who traveled in the same circles as Charlotte did assumed that she was a young woman of wealth and breeding who was enjoying dating a variety of influential men before settling down, marrying, and having children. It was a period almost fifty years ago and no one thought she was having sex with her "dates." She was too prominent, well-bred, and every inch a "lady." When she dropped out of the social whirl at age twenty-seven, it was presumed that she had fallen in love.

But there was no announcement in any of the papers. There was nothing to indicate which man had been fortunate enough to gain her hand. Instead, Charlotte had become a madam, taking young women with what was called the right mix of "breeding, looks, education, and stupidity," then molding them into world-class prostitutes.

Charlotte had rules that had to be followed. Underwear had to be white and spotlessly clean at all times. Later she would expect a woman to wear underwear once, then discard it so she would in no way fail to have the correct image.

Purses had to be orderly and limited in what was carried. She felt that a messy purse was upsetting to a man and this might detract from a woman's being the perfect date.

Drugs and alcohol were taboo. The women were expected to stay sober so that they could be at their best. Drinking with the date had to be in moderation, and a woman would be fired instantly if she was reported to have lost control of herself.

Drugs were forbidden, though that rule was bent with some of the clients. For example, one Arab leader paid Charlotte ten thousand dollars each for five women at a time (half the money went to Charlotte, who covered expenses, and half went to her girls). The man was impotent but loved to watch the women having sex together. He also enjoyed giving them cocaine while they relaxed in one of his houses. Most of the girls took the drug, though none was an addict or became addicted.

Charlotte kept close files on all her customers and matched them with the women who worked for her. She noted which of the women played musical instruments, which were conversant about art, politics, or any other subject that might be important to the men paying the bills.

The women were expected to be treated properly, though almost anything was permitted within the privacy of the man's home or hotel suite. He could ask the girl to do anything to him, and he would be permitted to do anything with her except cause her pain or disfigurement. He could also provide her with clothing—sexy lingerie, costumes, etc.—but he could not ask her to bring such clothing. She had to be properly dressed at all times, carrying nothing additional with her. Thus he might request that the woman arrive in a low-cut, revealing, but socially "proper" evening gown, a cocktail dress, a business suit, or anything else that would be fitting. But anything else would be his responsibility.

The woman could refuse to return to a client if what he requested bothered her, though so long as it did not fit one of Charlotte's taboos, she could not refuse the first time if she agreed to the job. For example, one woman was sent to be a part of the fivesome hired by the Arab leader, found the situation personally disgusting, and refused to go back. Charlotte simply noted her refusal and arranged for the woman to go only with men who wanted a single woman.

The fees for the work were extremely high. Fifteen hundred dollars as a base price was considered fairly low. Twenty-five hundred dollars was a fairly frequent charge. Yet for the money, everyone was protected.

For example, health records were kept on both the women and the men, and the women had to submit to regular medical exams and blood tests. Not one of the women involved was able to remember a single incident when she or anyone she knew who worked for Charlotte had ever experienced a venereal disease. No one was exposed to AIDS. And any man who was suspected of using women who might be of lesser quality Charlotte dropped from the client list so her women would be protected.

A woman who lacked proper clothing for socializing with a head of state, a multimillionaire, or some similar client was taken on a shopping trip to the finest stores. Charlotte made certain that her women were always properly attired.

There were age limits for Charlotte's women. No one could work when she was more than twenty-seven years old, though there was no explanation for the cutoff point. Charlotte may have felt that the men preferred younger women, though some of the clients were known to personally date older women. She may have felt that there was a risk of the women becoming jaded after too many years working as prostitutes. Whatever the case, Charlotte's "retirees" left with large nest eggs if they were at all frugal.

The women who worked for Charlotte had varied reasons for doing it. Most common was the woman who had been sexually active, involved with bad relationships, in need of money, and with no sense that her life would ever improve with her current surroundings. "I was giving it away. Why shouldn't I get paid for it? I had no special feelings toward any man. The money was more than I could make any other way. I mean, there was no reason why not."

Charlotte's prostitutes received, in effect, a finishing school training in diplomacy, grooming, conversation, and sex. They were almost American geishas, trained for pleasure and companionship with men who were at ease determining the fate of nations. They were also somewhat self-centered, desirous of money, and with a low enough sense of self-worth to subvert any desire for personal success in exchange for the benefits the rich could offer. As a result, they were the ideal women for long-term relationships with some of the men who wanted such an arrangement.

The "sale" of a woman was never obvious. She was not treated as chattel. She was not stripped naked, chained, and placed on an auction block.

Instead, money changed hands, a plane ticket was provided, where necessary, an apartment, house, or estate obtained, clothing purchased, and other luxuries procured. Then the woman moved into the new environment, still appearing in public with the man, still engaging in whatever form of sex he desired, if any (always observing Charlotte's taboos), and living much as she had during the hours they were together in the past. The difference was that this time the plane ticket was for a one-way trip. The woman would be staying and Charlotte's share would come only from the initial agreed-upon fee.

How long the arrangement worked would vary with the needs and desires of the man. Some committed for the long term, with the couple staying together for five years, ten years, even longer. Some men discovered that familiarity was boring. After a few weeks they would find that they longed for the excitement of hiring additional women. They might still keep the woman "purchased" from Charlotte, but their interest would wane and it would only be a matter of time before she was asked to leave. And a few found that the woman fit into their circle of friends so nicely that when the desire for companionship ended, another male in that social set would court, then keep the woman. These latter circumstances followed very much the pattern of kept women who had not worked as prostitutes.

How a woman ended up depended upon the woman. She might eventually return to prostitution, marry, or continue as a kept woman as she met new men with wealth enough to pay her way. Much was determined by her standards, desires, and the men she met.

Elena varied from Charlotte in that she maintained the fiction that her arrangements were different. Elena enjoyed having parties three or four times a year. To these parties she would invite models, actresses, beautiful socialites who seemed eager for adventure, and other potentially willing women. All of them had beauty, enough money and training to be able to dress attractively, and enough intelligence to fit in with the men who would be coming to the party. Often mothers would encourage their daughters to go see Elena to try to obtain an invitation. They took pride in the relationships their daughters formed there and were as pleased as they would be if their daughters were going to a coming out party when the daughters attended the events.

The men were also carefully selected. Some were married. Others were not. Marital status did not matter so long as the man was rich and had a history of squiring beautiful women.

The parties were held in Elena's mansion, where the finest food and drink were catered for the event. Everyone was encouraged to mingle, all the men and most of the women knowing that they were auditioning for relationships for the next few months.

The pairing would be done quietly. Couples would talk, becoming attracted to each other or not. They would mingle, perhaps making a date to see each other again, occasionally leaving together to go for a drink somewhere private. It was all very discreet, very sophisticated. And when the man made his choice, Elena would receive her money.

Only a few of the international madams were located for this book and there were limits as to what they would discuss. However, they did explain how they obtained the women who were sent to men throughout the world.

"I look for the ladies who lunch," reported one madam. "I want someone with looks, breeding, and not too many smarts.

"She's got to have intelligence. Don't get me wrong. Men don't pay me my fees for bimbos. But she can't have drive and ambition. I don't want someone who is working in a career field. I want the young woman who is content living on her inheritance from Daddy or maybe calling herself an actress or model, yet not really being involved with the business.

"Most of what these women do is ornamental and quite boring. They sit around a yacht or swimming pool. They look glamorous in an expensive restaurant or at some party. Maybe there's some thrill the first few times you meet a head of state, a top movie actor, or some ultrarich investor, but that gets old fast. After a while the woman is supposed to be beautiful, good in bed, and heard when spoken to. Anyone with real ambition is not going to make it. She'll get bored too soon and she'll show it.

"I want women who will fit in with this world, and the ones you see hanging around the Polo Lounge [in Los Angeles], Ma Maison, and the other watering holes are the right type. I will often approach them about working for me, usually using one of my girls to make the contact. Once they relate to my girls, they can relate to the work. If I go up to them, I'm guilty of soliciting and we certainly can't have that."

While wanting similar profiles in the women who work for them, other madams prefer to have referrals from women with whom they are currently working. "They know the life. They know the excitement and the demands of this kind of work. They know what will be expected of them, the money that can be made, and they're still naïve enough to be excited by it all, to think it will never end for them."

It would seem that the madams are in the perfect position to black-mail both the women who work for them and the men who are the clients. Some of the kept women marry, usually extremely rich men who do not want others to know that they met their wives through a madam or that their wives ever did such work. Blackmail would seem natural, yet it is not done. Even when the madam goes into retirement so that such blackmail will no longer affect her future business, this does not seem to occur.

The one exception is part of a drama being played out at this writing. A top madam was arrested, though it is doubtful that she will go to trial. She requested that the charges be dropped and that she not be ha-rassed, but the prosecutor felt that she should not be considered above the law. Her home and office were searched, investigators seeking her "trick book," the record of her clients and their special interests.

The madam was so irate that she has now threatened to disclose the names of her clients. Her "trick book" has successfully been kept hidden, though she has told investigators that it includes the police chief of the city of where she was arrested, U.S. senators, men con-nected with the Reagan White House, and other equally prominent individuals. She is essentially holding the clients up to blackmail in order to protect herself from further prosecution.

Yet even with the risk, some men continue to seek women through the madams. These women, unlike conventional prostitutes, are gen-erally subject to careful health checks and blood tests before they see a client. They may or may not use drugs (some madams forbid it) and they may or may not be more sexually versatile than the average person (madams will keep records of the types of sexual requests made by the clients and find women who are willing to indulge such wishes). Most important, the women are expected to neither look nor act like pro titutes, their image being one of sophistication, intelligence, glamour, with their brains not to intrude at the wrong times.

Yet no matter how women become kept, the realities are the same. Some talk as though they are the mistresses or the girlfriends of the men who are keeping them, making the traditional comment, "I'm the one who is always alone on weekends and holidays." They become martyrs to the relationship, ever "understanding" about the reasons a divorce is impossible ("She is Catholic and takes the marriage vows very seriously, even though the marriage has fallen apart." "We can't do anything until the children are on their own. It would be too devastating for them to come from a broken home." "A divorce would kill my/her father/mother/grandparent." "This is a community-property state. I couldn't survive financially if we divorced and had to sell everything.").

Others claim they like the arrangement. They talk about the pleasure of good sex, pleasant companionship, nice surroundings, a living allowance, and many hours and/or days of privacy when they can enjoy being alone.

Yet the truth for all kept women is that they are unable to commit to a relationship.

"I never gave a relationship a chance," said Noreen. "I was so afraid that the man would find the real me that I did everything I could to prevent intimacy. I never let him truly know me because I thought that he would reject me. I manipulated him with sex, trying to be the best possible bed partner I could imagine. I did anything he wanted, hating him and fearing his rejection at the same time. I refused to talk openly about my feelings, and when I thought I was becoming vulnerable, I began looking for the next relationship.

"Commitment meant rejection because he would discover how worthless I am. I was a beautiful shell, a doll he could play with so long as he didn't try to look inside. I didn't dare let anyone truly get to know me because I was terrified that he would just confirm what I already knew about myself."

Self-hate, a lack of a sense of self-worth, and similar factors all prevent commitment. However, there is also the opposite, the "spoiled brat" who feels that she deserves to be kept because of her beauty, brains, and the way in which she was raised. While psychologists have found that such a woman is likely to prove to have been emotionally abused and hurting in the same way that I was when growing up, during her first few years as a kept woman, it is the arrogance that prevents commitment.

"I never cared about getting to know a man," said Antonia. "I wanted attention, gifts, adoring looks, and embarrassingly hard cocks whenever I entered a room. I was delighted when a man learned about me, about my likes and dislikes. I was flattered when he would try to draw me out, learn where I was vulnerable, provide me with gifts he knew I would like, touch me in all the right places, arrange for me to have my favorite foods. I was like a queen bitch with men as my loyal subjects. There was no way I could have someone else in my life with that type of attitude, though I thought I was deliriously happy at the time."

The nature of the kept relationship prevents commitment. The men are married and cheating on their wives or involved with more than one woman at a time. The women may be angry, self-centered, manipulative, and/or filled with self-loathing. There are usually psychological problems related to past rape or sexual molestation. There are unresolved difficulties with previous relationships. And almost always there is a reluctance to go for counseling because the end result of that is change and change is an unknown most of the kept women fear while still within the life-style. They are completely out of control, yet they talk as though they are in control, suppressing their true feelings so long as they can play the game.

6

The Happier Side of Being Kept

"I considered it a two-year vacation," said Germaine. "I was working in one of those jobs where the glamour and the perks outweighed the money.

"I don't know what you'd call my title at the advertising agency because the job was better than a gofer position. I was what the agency called a creative assistant, which means that I had responsibility for some minor campaigns, had to shepherd other people's work through the various development and production processes, and traveled to a lot of client meetings, where I did whatever had to be done. Still, if someone had to go for coffee, I was the one to do it. And my pay . . . Well, let's just say that I had a studio apartment furnished in early Goodwill Industries and a charged-to-the-limit credit card.

"Anyway, we had this one client. You'd know his name if I told you. He's a big, rather fat man who looks like he'd be perfect in the role of one of those cigar-chomping, back-room politicians from the turn of the century. Yet he didn't smoke, limited his drinking, and actually looked quite attractive in his clothes, something that surprised me about someone his size. He was also head of one of those conglomerates that produces everything from frozen foods to electronics. It seemed that he

135

must have been over a hundred different companies, but whatever the case, he was increasingly using our agency.

"I met the man, I'll call him Sam, in Chicago where we had a regional meeting of some of his holdings that we handled. I was there to take notes, look attractive, fax copies of documents to the New York office, make a few creative suggestions, then blend into the background until someone came up with some sort of busy work for me to do. Still, there were few enough of us at the meeting that we all were invited to some banquet the executives were having to celebrate the tenth anniversary of one of the companies they owned.

"I was seated across from Sam during the dinner. We began talking about all manner of things. We both love pre-Columbian art, Chinese silk screens, and Japanese monster movies. I mean, how could you find two better-suited people than that?

"I thought it was going to be a delightful evening and nothing more. Even that would have been a bonus considering how unimportant I was to the agency and how dull most of the meetings had been, everybody stroking everyone else and little of substance being accomplished. Yet the next morning there was a beautiful bouquet of flowers surrounding an expensive bottle of champagne delivered to my hotel room. There was also a request that I have breakfast with him at the corporate facility in his regional headquarters office. Naturally I accepted.

"Things began moving rather rapidly after that. He made it clear that he was married and that our relationship was strictly business. He said that I was young, attractive, and delightful company. He asked if I would mind working from their corporate offices instead of my New York base because he would like to have me around. I was flattered, had no attachments other than my apartment, and agreed to make the change.

"I don't know when things changed between us or if they ever did. I think maybe we both knew from that first night just what was happening. He was looking for a companion and I was looking for . . . I don't know what. Not him, certainly. At least not so far as looks were concerned.

"Thinking about it, the looks I mean. It's a funny thing about the men. Most of the really attractive ones aren't handsome by any means. They're not even what I would call good-looking. They're better than handsome. They're self-assured. Like Sam. He was fat and underexercised. He wore expensive clothing that was custom-tailored because it fit him better than anything else, but that was his only concession to vanity. Other than being clean, he didn't care what type of impression he made. He was always in good taste, his clothing appropriate for the occasion, but he wasn't trying to impress anybody. It was as though he walked around saying, 'Here I am. Like me or not. But what you see is what you get.' Do you understand what I mean?

"And I found that incredibly sexy. I was young and all the men I dated were wrapped up in themselves. They were runners or worked out at health clubs. They had their hair styled and when you went into their bathrooms, they had more styling mousse, creams, blow dryers, and God knows what else than most women I know have. I even knew one guy who kept a comb by the bed when he had sex so that the minute he came, he could straighten his hair. I think he would have worn a hairnet to bed if he had thought of it.

"So here was this older, rich, powerful man who didn't give a damn about himself, who was incredibly smart, funny, and interested in me. I was flattered.

"Not that I hadn't been respected before. I know how I must sound talking about my job and all, but the truth is that it was surprisingly responsible. It was the kind of job where you learn a little about everything, they see how much you can handle, then they keep moving you up. I was on the fast track to account executive with management potential, so I knew that what I was experiencing was really short-term. I'd eventually be making good money, have real responsibility, and achieve what I wanted.

"I was also secure with myself. I came from a really loving family where my parents were extremely supportive. They kept telling me that I had to crawl before I could walk, but they made it seem like if I went slowly, I could do anything.

"Actually, they weren't all that thrilled with Sam because they thought I was getting into something over my head. I couldn't tell them that I was just going to have fun because they were certain I was going to get hurt.

"The company arranged for me to have an apartment that was close at hand, a place that cost as much as my net income when I was working in New York. I was told that such arrangements were 'standard' when someone was brought to Chicago for short-term work and I went along with that myth. But the place was fully furnished for me, including a

VCR and several videotapes of the Godzilla movies. Now you know that's not part of any deal. That had to come from Sam who knew I loved those dumb monster pictures.

"There never was much sex with Sam. I think he felt like he was cheating on his wife the three or four times we went to bed together during the two years he kept me.

"I didn't really understand it. I was taken to numerous affairs there, and though his home was out of state, he maintained a place with his wife on the Gold Coast and she often was there with him. They were even photographed together at charity benefits, yet he had no qualms about escorting me publicly, introducing me as an assistant. I don't know how he juggled everything and I don't care. There was never any scandal, never any obvious effort to avoid our being seen or photographed together.

"The two years were marvelous. We eventually traveled together to Atlanta, Houston, Cleveland, Beverly Hills, Toronto, London, Paris . . . We went in the company plane and stayed in the company hotel suites they arranged. We almost always had separate rooms because, like I said, sex was never important to him. The few times we were intimate, he had no trouble. In fact, even though his size was kind of a turnoff at first, he knew all the right places to touch a woman and it was better than with a lot of the studs I had known. But I think he had this rather odd moral code. He could keep me, but he couldn't sleep with me. Keeping me was business. Sleeping with me was adultery and he wasn't comfortable with that.

"Things kind of came to an end after a while. I was offered a fabulous job in Dallas and decided to take it. Then I met this man who could offer me absolutely nothing but himself, and I mean a hundred percent of himself. He knew I dated Sam, but he didn't know I was kept by him. He wouldn't have understood the shallowness of the whole thing.

"Bill, my fiancé, is a veterinarian, if you can believe that. He makes about a thousand dollars per week and really doesn't have a future that's going to be much different. But he's a truly decent guy who absolutely adores me, and I like that quality in a man.

"No. Seriously. Bill represents love, marriage, happiness and probably a lifetime mortgage on a house that's never quite big enough. Sam represents more money than anyone has the right to imagine, world travel, presents, and a lot of fun. But there was no commitment, not to me, not to his wife. I had my fling and I'm ready for a real relationship. Even my parents are relieved."

As Germaine can attest, there can be positive experiences among kept women, though even these have their odd twists. For example, there is Prissy, an actress who's never starred in anything but appears regularly in films with enough lines to be the envy of the less employed among Hollywood hopefuls. She managed to be kept by an older Hollywood star who earns many millions of dollars, both from his current productions and from residuals from past work. He also has enough investments in a variety of businesses to be worth in the neighborhood of three hundred million to five hundred million dollars.

"God, I loved it," said Prissy. "This guy had a yacht on which he liked to throw theme parties. One time he had everyone dress like they were out of the *Arabian Nights*. I had this really sexy harem costume custom made for me. It was all silk and real jewels, and it fit me perfectly. I don't know what he paid for it all, but he let me keep it and the jewels alone were appraised at ten thousand dollars when I took them to Tiffany's to see if they were real.

"He had these really big guys, they looked like linebackers for some pro football team, wearing little more than jockstraps and turbans, standing around with giant palm fronds. I got to recline on silk pillows while one of the 'Nubian slaves' fed me beluga caviar and gave me sips of Dom Perignon. There must have been a hundred guests, and more than that number in help, to really make that thing decadent.

"Another time he threw a party in memory of the nineteenth-century tycoons. All the men got big Havana cigars wrapped in hundred-dollar bills which they were expected to use to light the cigars. He modeled it after something he had read that the Vanderbilts or the Rockefellers or one of those families had done around the turn of the century. He even commissioned a period dress for me.

"The whole thing was exciting, but it wasn't real life. Everyone was playing and I was just part of the fun. I socked away some of the gifts and stayed with him until I got bored.

"Eventually I found a man I really love. He's poor, unfortunately, but it's amazing how easy it is to adapt to poverty when you love the man. He's a corporate lawyer who knows how to make billions for his clients but he'll never be rich himself. So I drive my car, don't have a yacht for parties, and no longer think about private landing pads for helicopters. I had my fling and now I have my happiness as well. I don't even miss the good life."

What she means by "he's poor" is that her husband, the attorney, is worth $3 million from an inheritance and earns $150,000 per year from his law practice. She has been reduced to driving her own car, but it is the top-of-the-line Mercedes-Benz with all the extras, including a telephone. They vacation in Europe and ski throughout the world. Yet by comparison, it is a comedown that many kept women could not have handled.

Ita also handled things in her own manner. She is a free-lance journalist living in the East who was offered a chance to be a kept woman by one of the subjects of an article she was researching. The man is a successful contractor with construction projects throughout the United States.

"He gave me my nest egg," Ita explained. "Look, I know it sounds crass, but I'm in a business where there are no vacations, no pension plans, no benefits. Trying to get health insurance was a real bitch and the costs will break you. I don't have a working spouse. I don't have rich parents. I just have a computer, a telephone, and a willingness to hustle my ass in order to get stories magazines pay me to write.

"I'm doing okay, but what if I want a break? What if something happens to me? I'm always driving or flying somewhere. I'm always reading for ideas and not for enjoyment. My life's hard in a lot of ways, though I love it and wouldn't change for anything.

"Anyway, so here's this guy, suave, Mr. Cool, you know? He's got the big house, the chauffeur, the corporate jet. He's probably mob-connected because, in doing the first story on him, I couldn't find any evidence of labor problems and that usually means the guy's connected. But he handles it well. He has the Mafia types keep a low profile if they are involved.

"So anyway, he takes me home one day and makes smart-ass remarks about where I live. I told him that I'd move to one of his buildings in a second if I had someone to pay the rent. He just said that maybe something could be arranged, then smiled that little boy smile of his. Jesus, he is a sexy bastard, even though I know he beds down half the women in the country when he goes on those trips of his.

"Basically he wanted to get in my pants. I'm good-looking. I work out at a health club, a cheap health club, but fully equipped. I haven't been a virgin since my freshman year in high school. I've been around the block a few times and I've got enough brains to be able to understand anything he says.

"Finally I let him do it. Hell, I encouraged him. I used every trick I knew in bed so that he was sore as anything by the time he went home. If his wife wanted him, he couldn't have gotten it up for a week.

"I figured my attitude would make him or break him. I didn't expect him to come back and offer me that apartment, fully furnished by one of those specialty shops that rents to millionaires. The apartment had the kind of furniture I didn't know if I was supposed to sit on or rope off with one of those chains the museums use to keep people from touching it. Even the paintings he rented for the walls were good original works by British nineteenth-century artists of enough renown to be intimidating. I'd like to earn in a year what those things cost. And they were second-quality. They weren't the artists' best.

"Anyway, I had the place to live, I had some really great sex with this guy, and I was going out to eat, getting new clothes, generally having the run of his platinum American Express card. I thought I was in heaven, though I still had to worry about my next sale. Even being kept, you can't be out of the publishers' minds for too long without their forgetting about you and thinking about someone else when good assignments come along.

"There was a point when he began feeling guilty about something. I never was sure what. Maybe he was having sex with his wife and was worried I'd think he was cheating on me. Anyway, whatever it was, he started buying me presents.

"Well, now I began to understand how to play this game. He wanted to buy me an expensive sports car, and I really did need a new set of wheels. I had a six-year-old Toyota that was beginning to threaten major breakdowns. But I didn't want the expensive sports car. What I wanted was a cheap little car and the difference in cash, but how do you tell a guy like that the truth?

"Finally I lied to him. I told him I had a rare coin collection and the sexiest thing a man had ever done was to take that collection seriously, helping me to fill it by buying an occasional good piece as a present.

"I was in Manhattan a lot, so I soon became a regular at Stack's on West Fifty-Seventh Street. I used their advice concerning long- and short-term potential. I avoided the common pieces and the fads. I got some excellent gold and silver pieces, a few early coppers, some ancients, some Canadian silver dollars, and some crowns. The crowns are dollar-size coins and they're quite beautiful. They're also in demand if you get the right ones from the right countries, and I had great advisers. I had never collected coins before, despite what I told him, but I had done some articles on investments and I'm a quick learner.

"I diversified a little. I got some good jewelry and some small antiques, as well as a couple of good paintings that I could own, not just rent for the walls. I don't know how much he spent in all, though it was at least fifty-thousand or sixty-thousand dollars, maybe more. All I know is that it was a nice diversified portfolio of collectibles and I socked everything but the paintings in a safe-deposit box.

"By the time we broke up, I had my nest egg and he had had a great time in bed. I gave him measure for measure, but I never saw anything permanent with him. I mean, even if he really loved me, who wants a man who cheats on his wife? He could have divorced her and then come after me if he was so in love with me. A guy like this, if you marry him, you're always going to wonder what he's doing when he's away from you. It's the kind of thing that could drive a woman crazy, and who needs that.

"Now I'm just looking for a nice decent guy who's unattached, rich or poor, and not all hung up. The collectible market shows a nice steady rise over the years, so I'm not going to get my legs cut out from under me like you might in the stock market. If anything happens to me before I strike it rich with some best seller, I've got something to sell that will keep me solvent for quite a while.

"Would I ever let myself be kept again? I don't think so. It's too much of a game and I don't like the way I am when I'm playing it. But, hell, if I had a sister in the same situation and she wanted to go for it, more power to her."

These were among the few kept women who reported good times, yet even with these there was a sense of underlying pain. As one formerly kept woman said, "It was like an adolescent game. I remember when we used to be possessive of our boyfriends, as though they were objects we could own. We'd get into jealous rages when someone else would try to steal them. Yet if you think about it, who wants a boy who can be seduced by 'feminine wiles'? An adolescent might try to use someone else, but not an adult.

"There's nothing nice about being kept when you're doing it for personal gain. I know a number of women who are hurting, who can't commit. But I'm not like that. I went into it for all I could get and I made a lot of money in a short period of time. I used the man and let him use me, and I don't like that part of myself. I don't know which of us was the more pathetic if I try to look at things objectively."

And there is the problem. I wanted to include the good stories, the ones of the women who had normal, loving, nurturing childhoods, who took advantage of offers that enabled them to see the world, then walked away and found healthy relationships.

The women mentioned in this chapter are typical of those who enjoyed such relationships. They entered the business of being kept with their eyes open. They took advantage of the perquisites, saved their money and/or gifts, and treated the entire experience as a lark, like a college student gifted with a year abroad. Yet in the end, it might be said that they were corrupted to a degree.

Keeping a woman is still a condition that holds emotional needs at a distance. The man is usually adulterous and always unwilling or unable to commit to another human being. In fact, the very idea of keeping a woman rather than either living with her as her lover or marrying her indicates his inability to make a commitment. He may be insecure, afraid of aging, or desperate for the approval of other males whom he thinks need to see proof of his potency. He wants image over substance in his life. He is willing to buy love, respect, and admiration.

There are only three ways a woman can react to such a man. She can ignore his advances, a common situation in the workplace. She can yield to his advances, enjoying the benefits that he wants to offer to reinforce his own circumstances. And she can act as a friend, helping him to gain a new, positive self-image.

There are few women who want to try and turn an ardent, wealthy suitor into a genuine friend whom they can help through his troubled self-image problem. The men do not seem to be worth the effort. There is nothing obvious to be gained other than what will probably prove to be mixed signals and a man who becomes even more intense than he was when initially trying to start the affair. More important, the man is probably married, so such an effort really belongs in the hands of the ongoing intimate partner.

Another problem with the woman serving as counselor is the fact that the man may have little respect for women. They may be objects for adornment and conquest, not friendship. The love-hate relationship he holds prevents the type of emotional intimacy needed for change.

This leaves the woman with a situation in which she is likely to take advantage of the man, if she chooses to get involved at all. It is an action that feeds off his emotional problems and insecurities, so is it possible that her acceptance of such a life-style is not as destructive in its own way as that of the woman addicted to being kept? The woman may survive. The woman may triumph when it comes to the acquisition of material goods. But the callousness of her action in knowingly using the man may be as harmful in its own way as being completely caught up in the life-style in the first place.

When it comes to kept women, the only "happy ending" is the one that occurs when she completely walks away.

7

But What About the Keepers?

Just as there are a number of similarities in the backgrounds of kept women, so are there likely family histories for the men who keep them. Some come from great wealth. Others have worked their way up from poverty. Yet they almost all share somehow similar psychological backgrounds.

"My father was an immigrant who took the promise of America very seriously. He was thirteen when he came to this country, the third son in his family to emigrate from Europe. He had little education and almost no money. However, he was certain that his older brother who ran a clothing store would give him a job, since it was the brother who sponsored him," said Joseph, a wealthy businessman who is working on his third wife and his fourth kept woman in thirty years.

"That uncle of mine told my father to go to hell. He said that he had sponsored him, but once he got here, he was on his own. He could sleep in the streets for all he cared.

"My father was angry about the treatment and determined to show his brother that he could be even more successful. He began hustling work, selling newspapers, doing odd jobs for bootleggers, running errands for the gamblers who hung out in the backs of smoke shops, saving his money, and using everything he could to buy seconds. This was a period when you apparently could pick up faulty clothing cheaply in the garment district, and my father found that he could mend it fairly easily. He became a self-taught tailor, repairing tears, replacing buttons, and generally making what was essentially a manufacturer's discards nice again.

"My father filled a boardinghouse room he rented with the repaired seconds, then saved his money until he could rent a small shop in a lower-income area of the city. He opened his own clothing store, selling what looked like expensive suits for a price the people in the area could afford. He did so well that the police checked him out, thinking that he was selling stolen merchandise.

"Eventually my father turned the running of the business over to a neighborhood girl he had met who was a skilled seamstress, even though she was only fifteen years old. She eventually became my mother, but he wasn't interested in marriage at that time. He was too busy trying to expand.

"There was a second brother in this country, a man who was in the scrap-metal business. He bought old cars, scrap from the steel mills, and anything else people brought him, then resold it somehow. I never really had an interest in that business, though I guess it was the forerunner of recycling. All I know is that my father thought it would be a good one to learn, so he left the clothing shop in the hands of my mother and applied to this brother for work. Again he was told to go to hell and again he found a way to go into competition.

"My father and mother were married two years later, and by then my father was becoming quite well-to-do. He owned two businesses and he still did some running around for the organized criminals he had worked with when first coming over here. Nothing serious, you understand. He was the bagman for some of the politicians, I guess, and he passed envelopes to neighborhood leaders involved with key issues or paid off the bartenders who gave free shots to anyone who voted. I don't remember just what. I used to hear the stories only occasionally at home, though they always fascinated me.

"I don't know when my father decided that he wanted to be rich. I had the feeling that there was a lot of anger toward his brothers, and being rich seemed to be his way to get back at them. All I know is that he got in the habit of using one business to get the capital to go into another one. They didn't even have to relate. His first two were different because he was trying to get back at his brothers, who had taken two different approaches to earning enough to feed their families. But he never was consistent. He seemed to sense which way people were going and stay one step ahead of them.

"Most of the grocery stores were small operations where you told the grocer or his wife what you wanted and they gave you personal service. My father was one of the early pioneers in what we now think of as supermarkets—larger stores, less help, more merchandise, and lower prices because of the volume and overhead differences. He had several stores, then went into banking and loan operations. The variety of his interests was amazing when I finally went over all his papers after his death ten years ago.

"You know, I still don't know what the point was. My father was never home with us kids. My mother raised us kids, kept the books for his businesses from home, and generally acted like a single parent. She was strong, almost authoritarian, and as penny-pinching as my father. We had more money than anyone would need in two lifetimes, but she forced me to wear hand-me-downs from my brothers and sister. I had patches on my clothing until I was in high school and grew just enough taller than the other kids that I had to have new things. Even then she shopped at discount stores and places selling seconds.

"I was also expected to work from the time I was a teenager. My mother didn't care what I did so long as I earned money. I was a caddie, a soda jerk, a delivery boy for one of the department stores . . . The only thing I didn't do much of was date girls because my mother thought that was a needless expense.

"My father was never part of my life, so he became the focal point of my life. I was angry with him for always being on the road. I resented his letting my mother dominate our lives so much. I thought of him as weak and was convinced that he hated us kids. I found out later that he thought that the greatest love he could give was financial security, but I never felt I had that. Since I saw him as weak and my mother as dominating my life, I came to hate them both.

"I guess that was why I was drawn to my first wife. She was one of those 'pretty little things' who seemed all perky and bubbly. Not really the cheerleader type. More the one who is always involved with school activities, decorating the gym, that kind of thing. She was quiet, laughed at all my jokes, was a good sport about anything, and seemed the opposite of my mother. She always asked me my opinion about things. She always deferred to me in any decision making. It was the perfect relationship and I asked her to marry me.

"I don't know when things started to change. I had taken over some of the running of my father's businesses and was branching out on my own as well. We had a lot of money and could afford a big house in the suburbs, which she thought was wonderful. She said it was a great place for all the children she wanted and I thought she was happy.

"Then I discovered that she was secretly taking the pill when I thought she was trying to get pregnant. I also discovered that she and some of her friends were going drinking and dancing every few days because they were bored. She said it didn't mean anything and I shouldn't resent her having fun when I kept myself so busy that I was never at home.

"One thing led to another and I realized she was constantly nagging, making demands, trying to change me. She'd blackmail me, telling me she might pick up some guy if she got any more bored. She wanted me to take her out more, buy her things, maybe get her involved with my business, even though she knew nothing about business and was terrible trying to work with others.

"Finally I caught her having sex with a friend of mine. They had been going at it for quite some time, I guess. I knew he had been a little distant, as though embarrassed by something, but I never suspected just what was taking place. Not until I caught them coming out of the elevator at a hotel where I was having lunch. She had a little overnight bag and the way she was clinging to him, there was no question about what had been taking place.

"It was then that I realized that a woman can't be trusted. You get too emotionally involved and you're just going to get hurt. I could understand my father's not spending much time at home, though I still resented the fact that he forced us to be victims of my domineering mother.

"I married again. In my business there are a lot of parties that have to be hosted, a lot of entertaining. It doesn't look right if a man isn't married.

"I chose a different woman this time. I chose one who had a career, a life of her own, who had no intention of changing. She came from money, too, and understood the importance of my image. We're friends of course, and compatible in bed, but this is also a business relationship for both of us and I'm more comfortable this way. I have my world. She has hers. And we're together when that matters. She's not the type who's going to hurt me again.

"I got involved with Sabrina because she's convenient. God, that sounds cold, but it's the truth. I mean, she's not the most glamorous woman I've ever known. She's a buyer for one of the department stores my company owns and I met her at a staff meeting. My wife was out of town, so I took her to dinner because I liked her ideas for revamping our image with a change in some of the merchandise she was handling. We really had a lot in common in the business and she had one of those minds that could understand fields beyond her experience. I found that we could talk about everything and that was refreshing.

"Don't get me wrong. I can talk with my wife, but she understands her world and I understand mine. We're both in business but the businesses are too different for us to really have much to say.

"Sabrina thinks like me. I can talk with her about something unrelated to retail merchandising, and if she doesn't know, she'll go out of her way to learn.

"I guess it started by my helping her out financially a couple of times. She was helping her parents and didn't have the money for a new car she needed for work. I arranged for her to get the car, then just paid for it myself, telling her it was a bonus for her good work. I meant that too, though I guess I wouldn't do that for some other employee.

"Then she was late for work a couple of times when the freeway traffic was too great, so I told her to move closer if she couldn't get here on time. She pointed out that the rent on the apartments near the office was too high for what she could afford on her salary. Since she was so valuable, I had the corporation rent her a place near to work, figuring she'd spend more time here if it was more convenient, and she didn't disappoint me.

"I can't tell you just why we went to bed together the first time. I guess it was just one of those things you know are right. We had been having dinner and talking and . . . I don't know. She leaned over and kissed me, and the next thing I knew we were on our way over to her place. I called my wife to say I was working on a presentation and would be home late, then ended up in bed with Sabrina. After that, sex just became a normal part of our life together.

"It's perfect because Sabrina doesn't want to marry or settle down. She likes her work and the traveling I'm having her do for the store. I also have her accompany me on out-of-town trips because I value her judgment and she makes an attractive partner. My wife can't get away that easily, so it really causes no conflicts at home. Of course, my wife doesn't know about Sabrina. That goes without saying. But the arrangement seems to be working out well for all of us."

The passive or absent father, the dominant mother, the bad first marriage—these are the three characteristics that seem common among many of the men who keep women. Rolfe was an orphan raised by a strong-willed grandmother and an equally powerful aunt. Eugene came from a single-parent family, where his mother had an answering service she ran from their home. Carlo essentially had no parents, being raised by the women on the staff of the mansion where he lived. His parents maintained residences in London, Rome, Paris, and Toronto. Neither ever seemed quite certain how little Carlo was born, but they hired a staff to take care of him. "I think my mother decided that she had accidentally picked up the wrong shopping bag at Bergdorf's one day and that's how they got me. The sex act seems so foreign to them, I can't imagine their doing it deliberately."

No matter what the background, there seems to be a love-hate relationship with the kept woman. Some of the women felt that the men who kept them were secretly bisexual or homosexual, yet had not achieved enough self-confidence to consider it. Certainly many are women haters who use the kept relationship for control and domination.

"It's the perfect situation," said Leighanne. "The guy has you exactly where he wants you. He gives you clothes, spending money, a fancy car. He takes you to fancy restaurants and buys you expensive presents. But he's always keeping an emotional distance. You can screw each other, but there's nothing personal about it. You get the feeling that there could just as easily be another girl in the same bed as yourself. You're hooked on the attention and the physical possessions, yet you know by his attitude that you could be gone tomorrow. You'll do anything to keep his interest and he takes advantage of that fact."

The common factors among men who keep women do not explain all their actions. Some men keep women for the long term, wanting the woman's commitment and not being concerned with the woman's changing looks or the problems of aging.

Lawton is a New York advertising executive who has been keeping a former fashion model for the past twelve years. During that time she developed breast cancer and had to have a radical mastectomy. The surgery was successful, there has been no recurrence of the cancer, and he paid for reconstructive plastic surgery so that her appearance would not be obviously altered. Still, she is not the "perfect" physical specimen that she was before the cancer operation.

"What do I care about something like that?" Lawton explained. "This is and has always been a class-act broad. Sure, I had the hots for her when she was modeling. My wife was getting suspicious when I started clipping pictures of her out of some of the fashion magazines, though I told her I was considering using the model for some ads, which was sort of true. Actually, I just wanted to have sex with her. It was kind of an adolescent fantasy, like some pimply-faced teenager jerking off while looking at the lingerie ads in the Sears, Roebuck catalog. I certainly never thought I'd set her up in her own apartment in Manhattan or be with her when she had cancer surgery.

"I know a lot of guys who dump their girlfriends every year or two, but I can't understand that. To me, whatever happens to the face or body is like a road map of that person's life. I think Bitsy's all the more beautiful for having triumphed over the Big C than she was when we thought everything was perfect.

"Besides, she's so grateful. There was a little tension growing between us before the operation. Bitsy was getting a little too independent for my taste. She knew the rules when I set her up and she knew what I expected of her. Then she got a little mouthy, complaining about my wife, talking about how maybe she was wasting her time being kept when she could have any man she wanted. She wasn't always ready for sex when I dropped by. She said she didn't want to go to some of the parties I wanted to take her to on the West Coast because she didn't like the people, the life-style. I was afraid I was going to have to dump her, something I didn't want to do, when she found that lump.

"Best thing that ever happened. She's convinced that any other man would have dropped her. Friend of hers, married, had the husband pack his bags when his wife went into the hospital. The guy was a jerk, but she didn't know that.

"It's been a few years and Bitsy can't get enough of me. I want something kinky, she'll do it. I want her to meet some client. There's no back talk. We've got the perfect relationship."

The hostility and pride of men who keep women is sometimes

mirrored in the actions of the women themselves. They fail to see themselves as abused. They place the man on a pedestal and try to conform
to his expectations, no matter how negative they may be. They will beg
for forgiveness for some infraction of the generally unspoken rules of
the relationship rather than analyze the situation to see if the man was
wrong. In their lack of self-image, they accept the blame instead of
lashing out at the person who may have been selfish, inconsiderate, or
otherwise wrong in his actions.

But not all the men are as selfish as Lawton. He is typical of many
men in long-term kept relationships, though most will express themselves in less crude a manner. However, there are other motivating
factors.

For some of the men who have a long-term relationship, what is
important is the fantasy of being kept. "I don't have to worry about
shaving while my wife comes in to take a shit. I don't have to deal with
snot-nosed kids, a leak in the swimming pool, or PTA meetings. When
I'm with Mary Anna, I'm master of all I survey. We eat out. We have
sex. We travel. And always there is respect, happiness, perfection.
None of the daily problems of life are thrown at me. I don't have the
telephone ringing because of a crisis in the office. Each day is like being
on some idyllic island where nothing matters, where problems do not
exist," said David.

"Sure, I know that Mary Anna has to handle a lot of things to
keep me happy. But this is partially a business arrangement. We've
been together so long because she knows what I expect and she
gives it to me.

"My wife takes our relationship for granted. She knows that in this
community-property state she and the kids will be provided for. She
takes a proprietary attitude toward me like any other woman would.

"Mary Anna knows we're playing a fantasy. She knows who pays
the rent, supplies the credit cards, makes the cash deposits in her
bank. She recognizes that so long as things stay perfect, I'm happy.
She also knows she's not the first woman to live like this with me,
just the longest. And frankly, I'm hoping that nothing changes
because I'd be happy supporting her until I die with all the pleasure
she gives to me."

There is a different type of attitude toward the kept woman who
seems to be part of a revolving door in a man's life. These are the men
who fear aging or fading potency. They fantasize that so long as a

young, beautiful woman is on their arm, they have all the virility, sex appeal, and status that they wanted when they were young. To them the woman becomes a reflection, as though when they look into her sparkling eyes, touch her unlined face, stroke her taut, sensuous body, they are admiring their own youth. They are again trim, powerful, the essence of maleness as promoted in our society.

"I don't like old" was one often repeated comment. "I'm not old, so why should I surround myself with those who are? I like young people, young ideas, young women. They give me life. They're good for my image."

"My wife's let herself go" was another typical comment. "Fifty years old and she looks like someone's grandmother. [N.B.: In most cases the men quoted here were grandparents, a fact this one conveniently ignored.] You don't just throw away someone like that but that doesn't mean I have to be seen with her when I can avoid it."

"When you've got what I've got, why not have the best. The young ones are easy to train and eager to please. And you know what they say about variety . . ."

The comments repeatedly reflect the fact that the men perceive themselves, in part, through the women they are with. And though they seldom expressed such feelings, it also seemed that they feared too great an intimacy, a reason for the frequent turnover. "You get too close and pretty soon she's complaining about the way you dress or the way you toss your things about the apartment. She sees you make an ass of yourself and she starts bringing it up whenever you argue. She gets to be too much like a wife and that's the time to make a change" was the way one man put it.

In all cases where interviews could be made or in-depth backgrounds learned, there seemed to be as much insecurity among the men as among the women they kept. But the fact that they had power, money, fame, and a willingness to satisfy the often desperate wants of the women they kept put them in control positions. They could mask any anger toward the women. They could hide their insecurities about themselves and about life in general. They could have lives that were filled with show, with glamour, and with sensual pleasure. And because the women on their arms brought envy from their associates, their life-styles added to their prestige among seemingly equally insecure, though rich, famous, and/or powerful individuals they encountered.

Previous sexual abuse experienced by most kept women creates a phenomenon that also affects the men. The women learn early on to use their bodies for protection. An incestuous molester or other individual who is close enough to the child to be able to abuse her repeatedly often will act kinder when the girl is cooperative. The more brutal molesters simply stop beating the child when she yields to their perverted requests. Others, feeling great guilt, will shower the child with gifts and special attention as a way of easing their own consciences for violating a taboo.

Frequently for a victim there is an identification with the aggressor, a common situation in long-term hostage cases. According to Dr. Martin Reiser of the Los Angeles Police Department and other experts around the country, it is not uncommon for a woman held captive for a prolonged period of time, whether she is abused or simply in a state of terror because of the unknown, to declare affection or even love for the man or men involved. There is a point where the mind establishes a new relationship to ensure emotional survival. The victim identifies with the aggressor in an effort to end the fear and pain. In the extreme, the victim becomes a seemingly willing cohort in crime, such as Patty Hearst became after she was kidnapped, raped, and left bound and gagged in a dark closet for a prolonged period of time by the group calling itself the Symbionese Liberation Army.

In the Hearst case, the liberty to move unfettered, to use the bathroom, to eat, or to even see daylight were all controlled by one or more men. She had to learn to please them in order to survive. For the mind, the path of least resistance is to eventually join with the abusers and become as one with them. She gained physical freedom, though she had been so emotionally devastated that she never considered escaping. She became a part of the group because, to do so, was "safe." While critics say that she was armed at times and could have left for safety, statements that are true, psychologists involved with the case note that she had been "safe" in her boyfriend's apartment when kidnapped. For someone so brutalized, the ultimate safety lay in being totally cooperative, a part of the aggressors.

This is very similar to what a kept woman has often experienced. Her sexual cooperation and even sexual manipulation keep her safe. If she can learn to not just yield to but find a way to give her abuser so much pleasure that she will not be hurt, she will do so. She may even come to think that men only want sex and, therefore, she can control all men through her sexuality and sensuality.

During some of the interviews we conducted separately, for example, Ted, while interviewing, encountered a few women still in the life-style whom he described as "touchers."

"The incidents usually occurred after I had spent considerable time going over their childhoods. I had been encouraging them to talk about their experiences growing up, experiences that frequently included emotional and physical abuse. Many times the women would go from acting hardened to the past, even arrogant about their looks, beauty, and what they said they 'deserved' from men, to crying almost uncontrollably about the past. Their faces actually seemed to change, growing younger as they talked, their voices rising in pitch to the point where a twenty-eight year old might look and sound like a frightened little girl.

"Then the women would regain control as we moved into their adult experiences. They would start laughing and joking again, talking about the men who kept them with what frequently was a sense of disdain. This was the point at which a woman would move close to me, touching my arm, resting her hand on my knee, moving her body next to mine, when, minutes earlier, as she had talked about the childhood abuse, she was likely to have been sitting as far from me as the placement of chairs would allow, often with her knees drawn up to her chest, her arms wrapped around the knees, looking at me yet seeming to protect her body.

"I did not respond to the change in body language and touching, though there were some women to whom I was so drawn that I felt extremely uncomfortable. Whenever it was appropriate, I mentioned that I was married and briefly discussed my wife. As soon as the women realized that I was not going to respond to their touching and that my comments about my wife were meant to make it clear I understood the signals but was not going to cheat, they would move back a bit. They always seemed a little confused, as though they could not be comfortable with a situation where blatantly sexual overtures were ignored. I kept feeling that I could put them down or take them to bed and either reaction would have been fine. But to do nothing except continue talking in the way we had been doing, playing it straight, working on the book instead of using the book as an excuse for a sexual milieu, that was an experience they could not handle."

In conversing with the women under less stressful circumstances than having to be self-reflective in an interview, they frequently talk about how they are sexually better than other women. They make such statements almost as though they are badges of honor, even though the truth is that they have no way to compare themselves with the other women. Sex and seduction become tools of control as well as ways to avoid pain.

8

Children of Kept Women

"I hated my mother for years," said Cassie. "She told me about my father, this rich, exciting man who jetted all over the world, yet she wouldn't let me see him. I had to read about him in *Newsweek* and *Time*. Sometimes I'd get a present from him for my birthday, but usually I wouldn't and, when I did, I suspect it was sent in his name by my mother or someone else.

"He had other kids. God knows how many, now that I think about it. But he had a family that used to get written up all the time living in one of those wealthy New York suburbs where they still ride to the hounds and dress for dinner.

"I used to try to imagine what it would be like to live with him, to have it be my picture taken wearing riding clothes and trotting around on horseback. Once I cut out the head of one of my school pictures and pasted it over the body of a picture of his daughter.

"I knew that my father wanted me. I knew that it was my mother keeping me from him.

"I called him once. Collect. It was from a pay phone in downtown Chicago. I told the operator that I was his daughter and I got right through to him. But he didn't acknowledge my presence. He said that his daughter was in the other room. He asked if this was a joke.

"Yet he knew about me. His name was on my birth certificate.

"I was heartbroken, but I never thought about blaming my father. Why should I blame my father? He loved me. I knew that. He had something else happening in his life that was causing the problem. It was the way my mother was acting toward him. She was turning him against me, poisoning his mind, telling him awful things that made him not want to be with me.

"I also decided that I wasn't good enough for him. He was involved with a number of media companies that put out some of those fashion magazines where the models all have the shape of a broomstick. I figured that maybe I could get my figure to look like one of them, then go to New York, show up at his office, and he'd not only take me to his home, he'd put me in a magazine and be oh so proud of me.

"What I didn't realize was that I had all the ingredients of anorexia nervosa. I had a bad self-image, I was angry with my mother, and I wanted to use eating habits to gain love. I began starving myself, taking lots of vitamin pills, drinking fruit juices, and exercising like crazy. I rode my bike everywhere, worked out at a health club, exercised at home, and always felt like I was eating too much. I got down to 93 pounds when my normal weight should be about 120 for my height and build. That was when I was hospitalized."

Anorexia nervosa, bulimia, fantasies about the father, these are all common reactions among the children of kept women. It has been said that the children of dysfunctional families create dysfunctional families. Child abuse will often occur for five generations before one of the victims stops being a victimizer.

The problems such children face are twofold. The most common is that an adult repeats whatever is learned as a youth. If beatings are common punishment, then the adult child tends to resort to the same discipline when he or she in turn becomes a parent. It is only the more mature person who seeks a different way to handle discipline than the methods learned when growing up.

The second problem children experience when it comes to having a mother who is or was a kept woman is that the pattern that affected the mother now affects the daughter. All the elements that created the kept woman in the first place have gone on to the next generation. The father again becomes a fantasy figure. Gifts are used as a way of expressing love. The mother is seen as the barrier to the child's having a relationship with her natural father. And women in general are perceived as competition. The daughter of a kept woman has been set up to be a kept woman.

For the son of a kept woman, the situation is different. How different we cannot tell because we found few sons of kept women were raised by the woman. Instead, the sons often became part of an extended family or were given up for adoption.

For example, Jonathon's mother was a seventeen-year-old actress being kept by a British actor. She had friends living in Europe who were older, married, and unable to have children. She gave Jonathon to them and they raised him as their son, letting him know that he was adopted and who his parents were. His natural mother keeps in regular contact with him and the two of them are friends. But he has been raised in a normal home environment, is healthy and mature. The arrangement is unusual but constructive.

Edward's mother, Lynnellen, was a secretary in the Boston area who was first kept by her boss when she went to work at twenty years of age. She was loyal to the man who was keeping her, claiming that the father of the child was a boy with whom she had gone to high school who was conveniently killed in a car crash shortly after the time she became pregnant. She had dated him occasionally in the past, the relationship never having reached that level of intimacy, but they were seen enough that both family and friends believed the lie.

After the birth, Lynnellen's mother cared for Edward. Lynnellen drifted away from the relationship with her boss and began going to parties, staying out all night, and generally acting wild. Her parents were concerned only about the child's welfare, taking care of Edward despite the fact that they were in their fifties and had planned for an early retirement. They had had foster children in the past in addition to their two daughters, with Lynnellen being the only one who had entered a "kept" situation, so adding the son was not unfamiliar to them.

Today Edward is twelve and considers his grandparents his real parents despite the fact that Lynnellen is his mother. The grandparents have custody of the child and Lynnellen retains a room in their house, a room she seldom uses. The boy seems well adjusted, though there is some tension between him and his mother, who alternates between expressing guilt and relief over the situation in which she finds herself.

Leonard is twenty-three, the son of an actress who was kept by the wealthy head of a major studio. The relationship ended bitterly when Leonard was nine, though he had never been close to the studio head, nor did he realize that the man was his father. He was told the fiction that his father was actually a soldier killed in Vietnam, and the boy's birth certificate bears the name of a youth who was killed in the war. The dead soldier was a man Leonard's mother had known, though she had never dated the man and never had sex with him.

There had been a number of benefits to the kept relationship, including an extremely large apartment and a nanny to take care of Leonard during those early years. The nanny was for the studio head's convenience, allowing him to have free time with the actress whenever he desired.

The breakup, when it occurred, was experienced with bitterness by Leonard's mother. Although she knew she was being kept by a married man who had a reputation as a womanizer, she still resented the end she had been expecting all along. She was allowed to stay in the apartment until the end of the school semester so Leonard would not be disrupted, then she had to find a place of her own. The entire incident angered her and scared her. She also came to resent the responsibility for her son that she had to bear alone.

Leonard never did understand his father. His mother told him that his father was patriotic and a war hero. His mother said he was a womanizer. And sometimes his mother said nothing at all. Although she never abandoned him, she spent as little time with her son as possible whenever she was in a kept situation. She chose men who could afford living circumstances that were large enough so that Leonard would not be in the way.

Eventually Leonard fantasized about his father. He created a life to emulate, deciding that his father would be pleased if he was active in sports, becoming involved with track and field. He considered joining the Army, but after talking with the recruiter decided that such a life was not for him. Instead he formed his own business, going to school part-time and working long hours. By the time he was twenty-three, Leonard was earning a low-six-figure annual income and is likely to become a millionaire within the next few years.

Leonard's sex life was where the parallels were interesting. He became engaged to a young woman he met at UCLA when he was twenty, the wedding being called off when she caught him with another girl. He explained that the affair meant nothing, an apparently truthful statement, yet his fiancée was too upset by his infidelity to consider giving him another chance. He was engaged again the following year, then broke up after suggesting that they have an "open relationship" after marriage to keep the excitement in their lives. Now he is dating two women and is notorious for having brief affairs. Friends say that he seems unable to commit to anyone. He is also quite young and may be engaged in what is called "sowing his wild oats."

Since Leonard refused repeated requests for interviews on any part of his personal life, we can only infer his attitude from his behavior. Yet his actions so mirror the typical man in a kept-woman relationship that it is likely he will follow his father's pattern, not from genetic traits but because of the emotional neglect he received while coming of age.

The one consistent pattern among the children of kept women is that their emotional growth and stability seem to be determined by the way they are raised. Most of these children are unwanted and their adult reactions to this are typical of unwanted children in any type of single-parent household. The fact that many of them become kept women themselves is not surprising since they have been raised with the same emotional experiences as their mothers have had.

There have also been incidents where a kept woman encouraged her daughter to engage in the same life-style. As Robbie explained: "I don't want her to get caught up in the nightmare I experienced, but Sarah has a good head on her shoulders. She's not going to fall victim to the abuse I encountered.

"Being kept is actually a positive experience. In what other way can a girl of twenty or twenty-one meet sophisticated, powerful men, travel the world, and experience the luxuries of life if she has not been born into great wealth? Being kept is like having a college education on life. She will see things and do things that will help her mature and develop a sophisticated outlook. She won't be one of those giggly sorority girls you see at the colleges, looking to do nothing but party. It's really no different than if I sent her to a finishing school."

What was unsaid is that Sarah had to go to a Minneapolis-based drug program to rid herself of codependency on drugs and alcohol at age twenty-five. She also was given herpes by an extremely powerful politician who knew he was infected but did not care that he was passing it on during one of its nondormant periods.

Sarah no longer speaks to her mother, which Robbie writes off as normal rebellion that all children experience, a "stage" she has to pass through. Sarah has gotten involved with a church program for singles and is trying to put herself through school while working as a waitress at an expensive restaurant. She knows that she has no future without training and resents the kind of education her mother thought would be good for her.

"I don't hate my mother," said Sarah when interviewed by telephone. "I accept her and forgive her. She did what she did because she couldn't justify her own actions any other way. She's weak and rather pathetic, yet I know I'm still too emotionally vulnerable to be around her and her friends.

"My minister teaches me that I have to learn to love her for who she is and I think I can do that. I also know that the life she introduced me to was an exciting one, a seductive one, that I could easily desire again.

"That's why I'm taking things one day at a time. I'm in a twelve-step program for recovering addicts. I'm active in my church. I'm working and going to school. And I'm trying to not think too much about anything other than what is taking place today.

"Hopefully someday my mother will find her own road to peace. Hopefully we will be friends. But right now I need my space. Right now I have to do what is right for me. Right now I have to put being a kept woman behind me, work out my anger, and take charge of my own life. I guess she did the best she could, but I wish that had been a little more than she did."

I suppose that I was lucky to not have a child to raise in the environments in which I lived. I can see myself handling a daughter in much the same way as I experienced, perhaps encouraging her to develop the skills that would win the approval I so desperately sought.

It's not a pleasant thought, especially since I still mourn the baby I lost. Yet it is a reality we all have to face if a child is born of the relationship. Without counseling, without the moral, religious, and psychologically accurate perspective we all need to get through life in a healthy manner, kept women breed kept women. It is the same problem as any other form of child abuse, though God knows we mean better for our children. We just become locked into an addictive pattern, and until we can break it for ourselves, it is nearly impossible to provide healthier guidance for our daughters and sons.

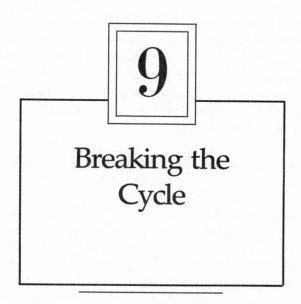

Breaking the
Cycle

I t is easy to look upon the kept woman with disdain. It is easy to ask why she is complaining about her fancy car, her glamorous clothing, her respected men. It is easy to ask why, if the life-style is ultimately so destructive, she does not leave.

The truth is that many women leave for a variety of reasons including because they have developed physical and emotional symptoms seemingly unrelated to their life-styles. Interviews with therapists such as Lee M. Schulman, Ph.D., for more than thirty years a Los Angeles area clinical psychologist; John Kappas, Ph.D., a psychologist in Van Nuys, California; and several others have revealed numerous reasons for changing the life-style. But these reasons will be discussed later in this chapter. The first question is why the women remain in the relationships at all.

Staying Kept

"Hope. You have to understand that I live with hope. I moved in with a man when I was seventeen. He was almost fifty, married a week in one of those relationships where everyone was high or stoned or stupid and marrying seemed to be the thing to do. He knew it was wrong for him almost immediately and we began living together when he had been with his wife for only seven days. Seven days . . .

"He didn't get divorced from her for four years. Neither of them ever got around to it. She stayed with a mutual friend for a while, then moved across country to where her family lived. And he began calling me his wife immediately. He told the reporters we were married. He introduced me as his wife. He wasn't trying to hide the fact that we were living together. He truly thought of me as his wife. We were that comfortable together.

"Eventually he did marry me. It was ten years later and we were constant companions. But I got my ring, my legal commitment from him. And even though he died less than a year after the ceremony, the experience taught me a lesson. If you want something badly enough and have the patience to wait for it, you'll get it."

Her name is Shanna and she is in a second kept relationship, a relationship she entered approximately three years after the death of her first husband/lover. This time the man is an independent businessman married to his second wife, an heiress. He has children by both wives and has impregnated Shanna twice. The first time she chose to have an abortion. The second time she lost the child through natural causes, the infant stillborn in the womb.

The businessman is not able to keep Shanna in the luxury she enjoyed during the early years of her previous relationship, but the emotional relationship is far stronger. She talks of having a deeper sense of loving and being loved than she has ever known before. She was incestuously raped and molested as a child, tolerating but never enjoying sex with her first husband. This changed with the businessman and she talks of truly enjoying intimacy for the first time.

Despite having less money, Shanna is not suffering. Her apartment costs more per year than she could earn from any job for which she is qualified. The businessman makes certain she has food and other necessities, takes her out to eat with some frequency, and helps her with spending money when he can. Yet he is never available when he is needed.

"He's with his son, who means everything to him. He's out of town on business with an important client and can't come back. He says he'll call at a certain hour, then gets tied up with something, or his secretary's around, or his son might overhear the call, or his wife's nearby . . .

"I had a miscarriage when he was taking a vacation with his family. I had to go to the hospital alone. I had to come back alone after the D&C. I had to go through the weekend mourning the loss and cursing him for not being near me.

"I live for when he's around and he tells me he loves me. He says he can't afford a divorce. He says he can't leave his son and he knows that his wife would get custody. He says it would be easy for her to find out that he's messing around if she wanted to pursue a divorce. He thinks she has a lover, but if she does, she's being discreet about it. And even if she does, she'd probably still get custody of the kid and that would kill him.

"I ache for him. I love him so much. He's the only man who ever treated me in such a way that I've known what it is to love someone else.

"I know I should leave him. I know I should date others, get on with my life. He keeps saying that he's afraid I'll do just that. He says he's worried about me getting fed up with the arrangement and finding someone else.

"But I'm not like that and I'm afraid he's holding back in our relationship because he doesn't want to get hurt when I leave him, even though I never would. I'm a one-man woman and I don't want anyone else.

"That's why I stay with him. That and the fact that I'm a survivor. I'm going to outlast his wife. I did it before and I can do it with him. I'm going to outlast her and have him to myself. I know it. If I can just hold on. I know it. The last man left his wife and married me. I don't see why this time should be any different if I can just hold on long enough."

"Time has a way of passing," said Sandra. "You don't let yourself think about it. Not in a negative way.

"I remember when my boss first moved me into an apartment near the office so we could spend more time together, we used to celebrate our little anniversaries. I got flowers and candy for our first week together, a special dinner in an expensive restaurant for our first month, a new car after the first year. I'd say to myself, 'He sees each moment as being precious. He cherishes the days, the weeks, the years.' What I never said, what I never thought, was that there went another day or week where the son of a bitch was two-timing his wife.

"I suppose it was all rather self-centered. I was getting what I wanted without too many demands. He wanted me and I reveled in that fact. The lack of commitment didn't matter because I probably would have been too scared to marry him or anyone, though I wouldn't admit this at the time.

"Eventually I noticed the occasional gray hair, but he called the hairs beautiful and said I'd be the sexiest old lady all the men would chase around the nursing home.

"I saw lines around my eyes and across my forehead. I noticed the puffiness that came from too little sleep, puffiness that hadn't existed before.

"And, of course, my job was different. I had gone from receptionist to executive secretary, a job that had the responsibilities and pay of essentially being a corporate vice president. All that took time, years of time, but my life was the same. I had a part-time lover, a part-time friend. My rent was paid, my salary supplemented, nice clothes, a new car every three years.

"Then I noticed something that began to bother me. My friends had gotten older, of course. Friends always get older if you live long enough, though you still remember yourself and them as they were when you were young. But their children. The babies they carried and I held when they brought them home from the hospital . . . Those babies looked like we did.

"I've got this friend, Marge, and she has a daughter named Simone. I was shopping in the grocery store and I saw the girl and I said, 'Hey, Marge, how's it going?' Then I realized that it wasn't Marge. The high school girl I was looking at, the dead ringer for Marge when we first became friends, was her daughter, Simone. An entire generation had grown up while I was being kept.

"God, that was sobering . . .

"That's when I began thinking about my life. I had been kept for almost twenty years. I hadn't dated, hadn't considered having children, hadn't considered that I would get old alone.

"And he had the best of everything. He was rich enough to take care of me for years to come. He would grow old fucking his wife, fucking me, living with a grin on his face and a commitment to no one. His wife would benefit from his retirement. His wife would benefit from his death.

"I mean, I had some retirement money and I socked away a lot of what he gave me. I even think he took care of me in his will. But I was going to grow old alone. My fondest memories were going to be of times with a man who cheated on everybody.

"Time passes. That's the only way to describe it. Time passes. We get into a pattern, a habit. It's exciting or comfortable or maybe just what is when we're twenty or twenty-five. And then time passes and suddenly you're forty, living the same life-style, doing the same things, still being kept.

"I can speak objectively, but you notice I'm still in the apartment he pays for. And I'm going to hustle you out of here soon because his wife's away for the weekend, so he's putting his home phone on call forwarding, then coming here so he can be with me and still answer when she calls. It's not over. I just never thought it would go this long."

To What Are They Addicted?

It is easy to say that kept women are addicted to the life-style. But what does that really mean? These women are not "love slaves" whose actions are worshipful of the men involved. They are also not addicted to the money because, if they were, in theory they would be saving more than they do. So just what is the overriding attraction that keeps them in a situation where they feel that they must be given what other people earn in their lives and relationships?

The answer, for many of the women, is self-hate. "I always believed that if I was lovable, my father wouldn't have left my mother the way he did. He abandoned the family and went to live with another woman who also had a daughter," said Naomi.

"I tried to be perfect. I knew that he liked the piano, so I insisted upon taking lessons. I practiced all the time, certain that if I played well enough, he would come back.

"I got good grades in school. I would go over to my grandmother's house, his mother's place, and help her cook and clean. I acted like a slave to her whenever I was there, determined to be so perfect that she would brag to him about me.

"And then, every once in a while, he would acknowledge something

I had done. He sent me a corsage to wear at my first recital. He even took me out to dinner once to celebrate when my softball team won the city championship one summer.

"Those few times of recognition were so precious to me, I found that I would do anything for an older man to get his approval. I had to be told I was good. I had to be told I was special. I had to be given a gift as proof I had done something well. Otherwise I was convinced that I had failed again in my life and that was something I could not do. I had been abandoned because I was unlovable. I felt loved only when the man would do something special for me. I was addicted to the bones of attention I received. I was addicted to the idea that he was giving me gifts, taking me places most women will never experience.

"I had to have that. To lose it was to go back to childhood, being unwanted, unloved, unlovable. I craved that special attention and would do anything to receive it."

Naomi's experience was quite similar to my own and those of the women Ted and I interviewed. We had no sense of self-worth and great fear of discovering that we might be as worthless as we feel ourselves to be.

There was always the magic appearance of our fathers or some other older male who gave us a sense that we had value. We lived for such attention, yet it was out of our control as children.

As young women we discovered ways to attain it. Since most of us had been molested or raped, we knew that our bodies could help us gain attention. We observed the men, found ways to please them, to seduce them into taking care of us.

The addiction was frequently to the attention we desperately needed. Because we hated ourselves, we had no respect for personal accomplishments. We downgraded our achievements, though we were so jealous of other women that we often postured and bragged in their presence to make them envious of us. Thus we needed the male approval and would go from relationship to relationship in order to constantly prove our value to ourselves. It was a hollow striving and the accomplishment was always accompanied by pain. We always knew that we had to be lining up the next man to keep us, preparing to reject our present situation before the man could reject us.

For a few of the very young kept women, the narcissism was overriding. Spoiled, self-indulgent, any pain they might recognize in themselves still many years off, they craved adulation.

"I wanted to see a man get hard when I walked in the room," said Hannalori. "I wanted to watch men making fools of themselves when they vied with each other to get me a drink. Just as I couldn't pass a mirror without glancing at myself, so I got high on attention from them. I needed the constant reinforcement of my wonderfulness by having such intense reactions from the men.

"I think that now I recognize the insecurity I must have had. I was an arrogant bitch, but trying to be objective about it, I was scared too. If some guy ignored me, I'd go out of my way to attract him. I wanted to be monogamous, kept by one man in a manner to which almost no one is accustomed. Yet I would periodically seduce one of the man's friends, a male staff member, or anyone else who ignored me. I had to have that attention even if I had to have a meaningless fuck be my measure of attractiveness.

"I thought of myself as some imperial goddess, addicted to the worship of others like an actress is addicted to the applause of her fans. But looking back on it all, I can see that I was really scared to death of myself. I know that there were even a few times when, though I wouldn't admit it, I fell asleep crying, clutching my pillow, because I feared that one of the men would expose me as a fraud. He would see that I wasn't so special, that God had given me what some people call 'drop-dead' good looks, though with nothing inside.

"Then I would look in the mirror and realize that such a fate could not befall me. I could walk away from it in a minute. I wasn't addicted to that attention. And then, satisfied, I'd go right back out after it."

There is one other addiction that the women have not mentioned yet I have experienced and seen in our conversations. This is the addiction to being with someone important to make us feel important.

I first realized this when talking with other kept women. I noticed that we were trying to top each other by bragging about the importance of the men we were with. We would talk about the acquisitions of major corporations, political conferences that were taking place, or an Academy Award nomination as though the achievement was one of our own. We did not give the men credit, even though they were the genuine achievers. We were taking the credit vicariously, living our lives through their actions.

Again this relates to our own insecurity and lack of self-worth. Many of us have been involved with acting and modeling, careers that make us high-profile before the public. Yet because we don't respect ourselves, we don't respect our work. We try to find our sense of self-worth through the achievements of the men.

I know that I was addicted primarily to power figures. I wanted men in politics and government, men who could affect the affairs of nations. I tried to be kept by them whenever possible, settling for the just rich only when necessary.

Other kept women had different attitudes. Some were drawn to actors, others to musicians, and still others were kept by corporate tycoons. They tried to stay with men who had recently made major deals, been nominated for Academy Awards, or were otherwise obviously at the top of their professions. But always they seemed addicted to the man's achievement in order to live their lives through his career. Certainly that was a factor in my case, and from the way the women talked with me, I think it is a factor in theirs. Yet, oddly, none of them discussed this when talking about the addictive side of being kept.

Breaking the Cycle

For Esther, it began with a stomachache. "Sometimes it was just a vague feeling of nausea," she explained. "Sometimes I had cramping as though the muscles were locking and unlocking in uncontrollable spasms. I didn't know if I had an ulcer, stomach cancer, or what. I only knew that I had to get help and quickly."

The internist Esther went to see could not find anything wrong with her, a fact that angered her. She questioned his competence, though he did not question the reality of her pain. Finally he agreed to place her in the hospital for a series of tests, all of which proved negative. There was nothing physically wrong with her in the sense that a precise symptom could be determined. It was decided to send her to see a psychologist to determine if there were underlying emotional problems that were revealing themselves through physical symptoms.

I broke the cycle when it became obvious that none of the men I wanted was willing to take me in on my own terms. In a sense, I had been abandoned by my father for the last time. I was in pain, in shock, suffering the humiliation of returning home to my mother at a time in life when I not only should have been independent, I should have been seeing my own child off into the world. I had no sense that life could be different. I felt myself a failure whose emotions had been laid bare for viewing by all the world. I wanted to die, to end my life, to go no further. I don't even know why I held on, talking with anyone who would listen, trying to maintain the façade of control while hoping that God's mercy would cause me to be the victim of a fatal car crash, a tragic house fire, an earthquake that would swallow me into the ground.

Yet I knew that I was alive, would survive, and could not continue as I had been. I had to find some answers, some alternate ways of coping. The past was over and I would never be the same again.

Other women told different stories. For example, Naomi began her breakthrough with depression. "It didn't make sense to me," she said. "I had everything I ever claimed that I wanted. I was working as a free-lance commercial artist. I drove an expensive Italian sports car. I had an apartment on Sutton Place. I had charge accounts at Bergdorf, Saks, Bloomingdale's, all the better stores. And I had money beyond what I was earning. Lorenzo, the man who was keeping me, put three thousand dollars into a checking account every month. That doesn't seem like much, but all my bills were channeled through one of his companies, so I never paid for anything.

"That should have been enough to give me the American dream, shouldn't it? I mean, I had it made. The trouble was that I couldn't shake this depression. Nothing seemed right. I didn't take any pleasure in anything except my artwork and you can't work on art twenty-four hours a day.

"One of my friends suggested I go see one of these Dr. Feelgood types who would give me something to pick me up. He did, all right. I don't know if it was speed or what it was, but I got hyper as hell, couldn't sleep, was anxious all the time, and I still felt depressed. Finally I found a shrink who told me to stop taking the pills and had me get to work on understanding myself. That's when I made my first break."

"I got too old," said Rena, a forty-year-old Chicago woman with a flawless face and figure. She looks five or ten years younger than her still youthful age and prides herself on the fact that she has never had cosmetic surgery.

"There were all these teenyboppers coming along and the men in the circle I was in liked the fantasy of deflowering virgins, though in some of the cases, I think the cherries were plucked when the girls were twelve, if you'll excuse my language. I had one man call me 'shopworn' because every man he knew had lived with me at one time or another. I was no longer new, exciting, or even a surprise. I knew everything about them and they knew everything about me. We had all grown too familiar with each other.

"I figured that there were only a few things I could do. I could move to some other city and try to start the game again, but at forty I was afraid that I couldn't get into the same money circles. I could drink a bottle of Dom Perignon, slash my wrists, and recline in a hot bath until I bled to death. I could change my name, leave the city, and get lost in some town where nobody had ever heard of me before. Or I could do what I did, which was to say, 'Screw this life.' I partied and was kept while I was young enough to enjoy it. Now it was time to get into the real world and decide what I wanted to be when I grew up."

"I fell in love," said Naomi. "It was really that simple.

"Being kept was a lark. It was like being involved in a campus protest over some inane thing or other. I mean, nobody took seriously what twenty or thirty students on an isolated college campus thought about apartheid in Africa or corruption in the Reagan administration, but we made placards and got our pictures in the campus newspaper and were all very smug. That's sort of the way being kept was like for me.

"I mean, here was this man with all this money who wanted to spend some of it on me. Getting one of those expensive toy cars that idles at seventy miles per hour to drive and having someone else buy the gas and insurance . . . I mean, the more he spent, the more erotic he became in my mind, so I really didn't mind sharing his bed when we traveled. But it just wasn't serious. The guy wasn't married, but he might as well have been. He wasn't going to spend his life with me. He didn't even know me. I was a face and a body to him. He didn't care what I wanted to do with my life, what I believed in, or anything else.

"Not that I wanted anything more. I felt like I was in school and I had this really rich friend who had all these neat toys she'd let me come over to her house to play with. I didn't care what the friend thought of me so long as I could keep playing with the toys in her recreation room.

"That's what being kept was like.

"Anyway, I met Richard through the guy who was keeping me. I needed to find a lawyer because of some problems my parents were having with the tenants of a small apartment complex they owned. They didn't know what to do, so I thought I had better find out. I was told that Richard was struggling but honest, so I figured I'd be going into some seedy little office with a guy who looked and talked like the actor Jimmy Stewart when he made all those Frank Capra movies. Instead I find that the guy is worth a million dollars and makes a low six-digit figure in his practice.

"Believe me, to the guy who was keeping me, a million dollars in the bank is 'struggling.' It's like some of the characters I met in Texas before the oil industry went bust and they had to sell the bank forty thousand acres. Those guys were so rich that they liked to talk about 'point men.' They liked to say that Joe was worth two points or Jim was worth five points. What they didn't say in that money-macho shorthand of theirs is that a point is a hundred million dollars. If you have just ninety-nine million dollars, I guess they don't let you play in their clubs or something.

"It wasn't exactly love at first sight. Richard was rather cold and abrasive at first. Later I found out he was completely turned on by me, a character trait I have always admired in a man, but he was afraid that I was out of his league. He knew my playmate, and though he didn't know the arrangement, when he discovered I had a few brains, he must have thought it was more serious than it was. Nice girls didn't get kept, or something like that. I don't know. I just found that I was turning to him for advice that I really didn't need, so finally I told him that I couldn't afford to keep coming to the office. I asked him to go to dinner with me, we began dating, and I fell in love. That's when I decided to leave the life.

Each of the women discovered the emptiness of being kept in her own way. Some developed psychosomatic symptoms that forced them into circumstances where they could receive emotional help. Others, such as I, were so battered by the truth of their existence that they were desperate for someone to tell them what to do or where to go. Yet, fortunately, in every case these women chose to seek help in one form or another. Most turned to psychologists or psychiatrists. A few went to clergy for counseling. Some simply put their lives in limbo, taking jobs, renting apartments, going through the motions of being like everyone else until they could begin to think about a different future.

As the next chapter will discuss, the addiction of being a kept woman can be conquered, but a minority of women experiencing this life-style are never able to leave. Some commit suicide, though frequently in ways that mask their actions. They may begin drinking heavily or use too many drugs. They are discovered passed out in the bathtub, their heads having slipped beneath the surface of the water. Or they are found along the highway, having lost control of their cars, the vehicles careening into telephone poles or off the side of a mountain. Or they may develop liver problems, lung conditions, damage to their hearts, with death coming as a result of their bodies' general deterioration. And some use a gun, poison, or carbon monoxide from their automobile exhaust to deliberately take their lives.

Others live a life of emptiness, refusing to accept themselves, their present, and their future. Desperate to retain the past, they exist as though in a time warp. Having lost the natural beauty of youth, they substitute cosmetic surgery and endless health spa workouts; they hide the normal lines of aging through facial makeup that eventually has the consistency and rigidity of aluminum siding.

What the aging, formerly kept woman forgets is that she has never been loved, never been desired for herself. She represented an image to the men who kept her, an image of eternal youth, virility, and desirability. A kept woman, to such men, is always as old as her passing years. They buy her as they would a set of steel-belted radial tires, knowing that she has a finite mileage which they must carefully check from month to month. Discard her after too long a time and their friends will criticize their inability to afford a replacement.

The kept woman, like automobile tires, is always interchangeable with dozens just like her. There are variations, of course. She can be blonde, brunette, or a redhead, just as tires come with white sidewalls, in black, or striped. But so long as she is serviceable, with a good mind, a good figure, and low mileage, she is a useful decorative asset.

The kept woman fantasizes that she has a unique identity, that she is special, that she forms an unforgettable period in a man's past. But just as a man is apt to forget when he drove with Goodyears, Firestones, Pirellis, or Michelins, so is he likely to blur Shirley with Yvonne, Hilda with Anne, Naomi with Amy. The names do not matter because names hint at an intimacy they are both unwilling to have and, at times, incapable of experiencing.

And so there are formerly kept women of fifty, sixty, and older who still try to visit the right cities in season. Their figures are easily the match of women thirty years their junior, yet their skin has the taut, unnatural quality that comes from one too many tummy tucks, face-lifts, eye jobs, and suctioning. Their hair is worn in styles that hide the tiny scars that remain from the surgeries that are as routine to them as the annual vacations taken by many Middle Americans.

The men are usually too gallant to ignore the women who once "shared" their beds and lives. They may give them a turn on the dance floor so long as no one thinks they are these women's escorts. They may exchange telephone numbers, then toss what they have pocketed into the nearest trash can and switch to an unlisted number. They speak with the same terms of endearment they used so many years in the past, though now they do it because they cannot remember the women's names. And when the next season arrives in Monte Carlo, they are traveling with yet another woman who is very young, very naïve, and certain that the life will go on forever.

10

So What Is a Normal Life, Anyway?

D r. Lee Shulman refers to the kept-woman life-style as an "addiction," a term that kept women themselves will use when they are willing to face the reality of their existence. Unfortunately, as an addiction it is often misunderstood. After all, how hard is it to adjust to having expensive clothes, a gorgeous apartment paid for by someone else, and all the spending money one could desire? The idea of luxury and comfort without work or responsibility seems to be a glimpse of heaven, not a preview of hell. However, what is not said is that, like any addict, the kept woman is completely out of control, reacting to subconscious drives that are dangerously self-destructive.

Dr. Shulman went on to explain that all kept women are the products of dysfunctional families. The least troubled women are the most likely to sustain relationships for many years. The most disturbed may be kept by a different man every six months to a year.

Fortunately, as with any addiction, the kept woman can break her "habit." The procedure essentially involves four simple steps, yet for reasons explored in this chapter, those steps often seem terrifying at best, near to impossible at worst.

1. Recognizing that the kept-woman life-style is both destructive and undesirable

2. Admitting to the problem when talking with others

3. Seeking information about the underlying motivation

4. Making the decision to change and pursuing that goal without unrealistic expectations

The low self-image of the kept woman that helps establish her destructive life-style pattern, the direct cause and effect of her abusive childhood, is readily understood. It is one of several forms of adult behavior that evolves from growing up in dysfunctional families. For example, women who are adult children of alcoholics, adult victims of child abuse, or have similar backgrounds may all respond with similar self-images. Some turn to drugs and alcohol. Some have an endless series of lovers or husbands. Some become angry, bitter, and/or depressed. And some become kept women.

Because of relatively consistent abusive backgrounds, the treatment they all need follows similar patterns. The most successful groups often utilize twelve-step programs such as that pioneered by Alcoholics Anonymous. Likewise, the greatest problem is what AA members sometimes call "terminal uniqueness." So long as someone insists upon feeling that he or she is unique, and thus not reachable through established methods, recovery may be impossible.

Kept women have deliberately held themselves emotionally isolated from others as adults. They have maintained a love-hate relationship with men, simultaneously being both manipulator and manipulated. They have also kept themselves emotionally isolated from other women, seeing the women as competition and, at times, as mirrors of their own lonely existence.

The result is that the difficulty lies not with diagnosing the kept woman's problem, not so much with treating her, but with her unwillingness to face the truth about herself. She fears that she is something bad. She fears that she is as worthless as others told her she was while growing up. She fears that her life will end when she is no longer invited to the right parties with the right people in the right countries. She is so terrified of what she might find inside herself that she does not want to look. Yet when she does make herself vulnerable, recovery is much easier than she might desire.

As is the case for an alcoholic, there are constant temptations and may be for many years to come. Like the alcoholic, yielding to the temptations can be self-destructive to a degree she could not previously imagine. Thus it is the internal war the kept woman experiences when she wants to change her life, not the steps that she must take to succeed in that change, that creates the problems for her.

The Dysfunctional Family

The problems that affect the kept woman who is trying to break from the patterns of the past have invariably started in childhood. It is rare to find a kept woman who has not experienced one form of abuse or another during her early years. This abuse may have taken the form of emotional, physical, or sexual attacks or it may have involved an attack against someone else because of the child's actions. One example of the latter type of abuse occurs when a man beats his wife because she has not taught her daughter to not spill her milk. Each time the child spills a glass of milk, there is a feeling of dread and responsibility for the fact that her mother is going to be battered by her father.

Emotional Abuse

Emotional abuse can take many forms and often occurs without the parents' awareness. This is because a child's understanding is very different from that of an adult. It is a simpler view of life with a sense of the magical. A child often believes that his or her actions can have far greater impact on the family structure than is possible.

For example, a child frequently feels that it is possible to influence an absent parent. This occurs when there is a death in the family, a parent who is a workaholic, a pending divorce, or a situation that results in the frequent absence or loss of the parent.

"I always blamed myself for my father's not being around when I was growing up," said Yvonne. "I was six years old when he was drafted and sent to Vietnam. I remember these soldiers coming to our house, my mother crying, and my grandparents coming over. They told me he had died, but I didn't believe them. I remember that the last thing he said to me was to be good to my mother, help her with the housework, and he would come back to play with me.

"I didn't understand death, but what I did understand was that somehow I must have been terrible because he didn't come back home. He said that if I was good, he'd come back to me, so I tried everything I could to be perfect. It didn't work, though. He never returned and I eventually came to hate him for dying like that. He lied to me and then abandoned me and I wanted to get even with him. I think I saw being kept as a way of getting back at my father, of manipulating men so they couldn't manipulate me the way I was certain that my father did.

"Sure, I know better, now. I know that getting killed wasn't his fault. I know that nothing I could have done would have prevented his death. But I was a kid, then, and no one bothered to talk with me about how I was perceiving things. We went through the mourning period and then we got on with our lives. Nobody, especially me, realized the anger and misperceptions I would live with for the next twenty-five years."

Another form of emotional abuse might be considered reverse motivation. The child is never good enough, no matter what he or she does. Instead of being rewarded for receiving better-than-average grades, the child is told that, next time, the report card should be perfect. If the child receives straight A's, he or she may be told, "I hope you can do as well next semester when the courses become difficult," instantly demeaning both the child and the accomplishment.

One girl was told, "You'd be so pretty if you would just lose a little weight." The mother felt that the statement was encouraging because she said that the girl could be pretty. But the message the child hears in such a case is "You're fat and ugly."

Another form of emotional abuse is to negatively compare the child with a sibling. "Why can't you be like your sister? She picks up her clothing. She is always helpful. She doesn't ask foolish questions." There may be times when both siblings are treated identically, each coming to see the other as a rival because neither understands that they are both being emotionally abused.

The methods for such abuse are limited only by the imagination of the family members who perpetuate the problem. One child may receive more gifts or more expensive gifts than the other for birthdays and holidays. Or the type of gift may be a subtle message. "My sister was given very feminine clothing for presents, lingerie, strapless dresses, really sexy things. But when I was her age I was given jeans, sweaters, practical clothing. My mother said that it was because I was the more practical one in the family, the one who didn't waste her time flirting and partying. But the message I got was that I wasn't attractive enough, wasn't popular enough to bother with such alluring clothing," said Cindy.

Sometimes parents, teachers, or family members decide that the best motivator is to tear down the child. "How stupid of you." "How could you be this dumb?" "You don't have a brain in your head." The words may be said in a loving tone or a humorous one, not necessarily in anger, but the child does not care. Words can transmit so much emotional abuse and the end result of hearing them may be a decision to give up.

Several years ago, one of the counties in Southern California did a study that revealed that when a child has failed in first grade, he or she is likely to eventually drop out of school. The teachers had been failing children to shock them, to teach them a lesson, or to challenge them to do better. They felt that giving F's at a time when it "didn't matter" would be a positive incentive for the children. The county's research showed that the action actually caused the children to give up on school and, in a sense, on life. Instead of feeling motivated, the children felt defeated. The action was extremely destructive, and changes were made in the school system to correct it.

Many families make the same mistake as the teachers did who failed the children. Their words and actions have a dead seriousness for a child which can result in a sense of defeat that is carried through life.

Physical and Sexual Abuse

Physical and sexual abuse are more obvious than emotional abuse, though they go hand in hand. Many of the kept women we interviewed had been emotionally abused. Many also talked of molestation or rapes in their childhoods, frequently by a family member. Often they would tell no one, either out of fear or guilt that somehow they must have provoked the vicious, hideous action. They had a poor sense of self-worth and often were willing to go along with sexual acts they did not wish to endure in order to please the man and not be turned away.

There are two types of physical abuse, and the type the child receives has strong impact on the child as an adult. One type, following misbehavior, is punishment of the child taken to an extreme. For example, a child is warned to be careful with a glass of milk, then begins playing, forgets the warning, and spills the milk. Instantly the father takes off his belt and whips the child. The violence is extreme, uncalled-for, and physically abusive. Yet it directly relates to the child's having done something wrong.

Such a physically abusive parent, if consistent, may do limited damage to the child. The beatings are severe and may constitute criminal child abuse. But if they are only for actions that are wrong, and if the parent either rewards good behavior or ignores it entirely, the child usually develops in a reasonably healthy manner. The child raised in such an environment will usually as an adult either be terrified of doing anything wrong, fearing violent punishment all of his or her life, or perhaps become aggressive. Such an adult may be determined to succeed at any cost, not afraid of failure and not willing to admit defeat. Both these traits have their good points, and the child with this type of abuse may eventually rise above the abuse, either with the help of counseling or on his or her own.

The other type of physical abuse is seemingly irrational and can lead to severe emotional trauma. This occurs when the parent is inconsistent with the abuse. The child may spill milk and be savagely beaten one day, then spill milk again the next day, only to have the parent act in a loving manner, hugging the child, giving the child a fresh glass and, perhaps, a cookie so he or she will not feel badly. The child never knows right or wrong because there is no way to interpret the parental behavior. This can lead to reactions ranging from a failure to thrive to hysteric dissociation, the technical name for what is often called "multiple personality." However this form of abuse is rare among kept women.

Sexual abuse may be incestuous or may occur with a local merchant, a member of the clergy, a Scout leader, teacher, or anyone else who comes into contact with the young. At least one in four women will not reach the age of eighteen without experiencing some form of sexual abuse. The ratio for men is one in ten, though some experts think that male child abuse may be the same as that for females, just less likely to be reported and more embarrassing to discuss in adulthood.

Many kept women we interviewed experienced some form of sexual molestation, not just the rapes that a number of the women described.

"I learned very early that I could get what I wanted by letting a man touch my body," said Tasha. "There was a momma-poppa grocery store near where I lived, one of those places where all the kids used to go to buy pop, candy, and ice cream after school. Right after I began to develop, and I got my breasts early as a kid, I noticed that the owner was paying more attention to me than to the other girls. He kept finding reasons to talk with me, to get me to stay a moment after the other children left.

"One day he made a physical pass at me, feeling my breasts for a moment and telling me how I was becoming a beautiful woman. I was eleven at the time and knew that what he was doing was wrong, but he did it so quickly and so casually that I could lie to myself and say there was nothing wrong with it. Anyway, instead of leaving when he did it, I smiled at him and just stood still until he stopped. Then he gave me an extra Three Musketeers, my favorite candy bar, and told me it was free.

"After that I realized that I could manipulate men into giving me whatever I wanted. I kept letting him cop a feel, getting free pop and candy, then making fun of him with the other girls. They always told me I was wrong, that I had no business letting him do it, but they were a little jealous because they didn't have the nerve.

"Then, when I was in high school, I kissed my guidance counselor. I had been goofing off, cutting classes, sneaking out to smoke, and he called me in his office. He warned me that I wouldn't be able to get a strong recommendation for the college I wanted to attend, so I tried manipulating him. I cried a bit, told him how eager I was to make something of myself, how I knew I had made a mistake in the way I acted in the past, and how I'd do anything to get another chance.

"I got real close to him, touching his hand, really making him uncomfortable. I had one of those sweaters that cling in all the right places and I knew he was watching my breasts. He got real uncomfortable, mumbled something about how he thought that maybe something could be done, and then I gave him a light kiss on the lips to thank him. He was stunned, sitting there for a moment before responding in ways he shouldn't have done. I just smiled, but I knew I'd have no trouble with a recommendation, no matter what my grades might be."

Tasha's experiences increased as she grew older. She came to realize that she could use sex to manipulate men. At the same time, she assumed that all men were not to be trusted. Drawn by the right sexual appeal by any woman, they would be unfaithful. By the time she entered the kept life, the early sexual molestations left her bitter, unable to trust, and determined to never emotionally commit to a man. She became a user because she had never known circumstances that allowed her to feel otherwise.

Rape, the most angry and violent of all sex-related acts, may leave a woman having thoughts and emotions similar to those of the individual who was molested as a child. A young rape victim, untreated, may reach puberty with a sexual awareness that is both more sophisticated and more naïve than those in others her age. She has experienced what she may think is the animal lust of men, not realizing that rape is a hate-filled act. She has also learned to survive by allowing the rape to happen, even though the first time or times she may have been beaten, restrained, or otherwise forced to not resist. She may hold men in disdain and choose to use her body to control them, a quality that is extremely important for the kept woman.

I mentioned that it was rare to find a kept woman who hasn't come from a background of abuse, and there is an exception: the spoiled, isolated child who is raised to think that the universe revolves around her. One of the women interviewed talked of being taught that she deserves the best. The men who keep her in wealth and luxury are merely giving her her due. Her comments are typical of a number of kept women, some of whom are actually hiding feelings of great inferiority, and some of whom actually believe it. They have become so conditioned to thinking that they are special, that the world owes them their pleasure, that they are actually immature, spoiled brats. However, almost always such self-laudatory, seemingly conceited statements reflect a false front and great insecurity.

In many ways, the kept women studied for this book are among the elite in our society. The majority of them are extremely beautiful, unusually intelligent whether or not they have had higher educations, and frequently quite capable. Many sought careers in glamour professions such as modeling and show business so that they could hide behind their looks, their talents, and, at times, a flamboyant stage presence. So long as they can keep others focused on superficial qualities or the part they are playing on the stage or in a film, they do not risk being exposed for what they think they really are.

There are other patterns as well, according to psychologists throughout the country who have worked with such individuals. And the most common, both for kept women and for adult victims of child abuse in general, is the inability to commit to a relationship.

There are different ways that the kept women entered their first relationship. Some, like me, married before being kept. Others entered the life-style right from the start. Either way, they frequently chose an abusive relationship for the first one.

The woman who has been a victim of child abuse seeks several things in the first relationship she experiences. One is an escape from that abuse. She wants to leave home, to seek anything that is different. She is certain that nothing can be as bad as what she has known. She will marry or live with the first man who is willing and able to take her away from the past. It is chance if he is a kind, decent, upstanding individual. She neither knows him nor cares who or what he is. Her concern is getting away.

Most likely the first relationship will either be abusive or completely passive. I married a man who raped me when I sought his protection from my home life. I went with the only person I knew, a man who had shown me the only kindness I had encountered from an older male. The fact that he raped me, that he attempted to have me experience a ménage à trois against my will, that he was obviously involved with others, never mattered. He was the best I was worth and I clung to him, caring about him for years later, even after he went to jail for crimes that hurt the lives of many others.

Many of the kept women explained that the first serious relationship they had was with men who would beat them when they got angry or who were verbally abusive. In several instances the women said that the verbal abuse was worse than the physical encounters because it played into their own feelings of self-doubt, inadequacy, and self-hate.

The opposite extreme is the woman who married a man for his weakness. "Norman was your classic nerd. He was a professor of ancient history at a major New York university and had inherited a sizable sum of money from an aunt. He was probably fifteen years older than me, a big age difference at the time.

"I told myself that I was fascinated by Norman's intellect and his patience as a teacher. I bragged that he would spend hours talking about ancient Greek civilization, making the past come alive. What I didn't face was the fact that he probably didn't know that Ed Koch was mayor of New York, that Studio 54 was no longer a hangout of the social elite, or even that Studio 54 had ever existed. He was entrenched in the past and would have talked for hours about it even if I hadn't wanted to listen. It was all he knew. Worse, it was all he wanted to know.

"I also liked the fact that he was always a perfect gentleman on our dates. He shook hands with me after a date, at least until I made the first move to kiss him. And he never tried to get his hands running all over my body like the other men I knew.

"The first time we made love, I told myself that I was reveling in the long, gentle foreplay. What I didn't want to admit was the fact that the foreplay took so long because he had trouble getting it up. He was a really lousy lover.

"I remember one time I went so far as to dress like Cleopatra and tried to get him to think of himself as Marc Antony. I thought it would be kind of kinky. Instead, he said I was too beautiful and went into a lecture about how really ugly a woman Cleopatra really was and how we know that from the portraits left on some ancient coins. Talk about a way to kill romance . . .

"But he was safe. That was the main thing. He didn't beat me like my father had. He didn't try to rape me, to hurt me, to do anything. It was easy to take a lack of passion so long as there was also a lack of pain."

No matter how the first relationship is experienced, there are certain consistencies among the women we interviewed that kept them from commiting. These consistencies too are found in the men in their lives in those cases where both have been victims of child abuse. They involve the need to protect oneself from the pain of rejection.

"I always felt that I was worthless," said Amy. "I mean, I put on this big act. I talked about how great I was. I often was driving some man's Rolls-Royce, having waiters treat me like royalty, having people look at me like I was a movie star or something. I bought clothing that showed off my figure and always made sure there was just enough cleavage so that I seemed modest, yet turned heads when I walked by. I read constantly so I could talk about anything in the news, no matter how obscure. I was the life of the party. I had to be. I was terrified that someone might not like me.

"The trouble was that every time I got serious about some man, I knew that there would come a time when I had to be vulnerable to him. I'd have to let down my guard. I'd have to let him see the real me and I knew that the real me was not worth much.

"I didn't want to be rejected. God, how I feared rejection. It was bad enough for me to know that I was garbage. To let anyone else find out . . . I couldn't handle that.

"So what I'd do is sabotage relationships. I don't mean I'd do it consciously. It's taken two years of therapy to talk with you the way I am. It was all subconscious and I was pissed as hell at the therapist when she started trying to get me to explore such feelings.

"Anyway, as soon as I sensed that the man was getting serious . . . I don't mean that he was keeping me. The fact that a guy is paying the bills or even living with me had nothing to do with his getting serious. It was when I knew he wanted more. Maybe marriage. Maybe a real emotional commitment regardless of the living arrangement. That was when I knew he'd discover what I was really like. That was when he'd know I wasn't worth having.

"I'd put him down then. I'd be a real bitch, tell him he wasn't worthy of me, try to cut him off at the balls, if you'll excuse the expression. I figured, better him than me. I didn't want to be hurt, so I went on the attack first. I didn't dare let him see the real me."

There are actually two common reactions for women who have the same lack of self-worth that Amy expressed. Some act as she did, taking the initiative to end the relationship. They may not be so harsh about it as she was, but they make certain that they are not the ones who are obviously suffering.

The other reaction is to hate the man. The ending of the relationship may be the same but the reasoning is not. When the man is hated, it is because the woman decides that she has underrated him. "I really admired him until I realized he truly loved me. No man who is worth anything could ever love me" is the reasoning used. "I must have picked a loser."

No matter why the woman rejects the man, whether because she fears he will learn the truth about her or because she decides that he must be terrible if he can love her, the end result is the inability to commit to a relationship. Every man has to be rejected. Every involvement is destined for failure.

Eventually one of two things happens. Either the woman tires of the kept life-style or she becomes embittered.

The woman who tires of being kept will often eventually seek counseling. "Why can't I find a decent man to marry?" she may ask. Or "Why do my relationships always seem to break up just when things are going well?" Or "If I'm so wonderful, how come I'm still single?"

The answers come slowly. Sometimes the woman goes to friends who seek to introduce her to available men. "You just haven't met the right man yet" is a typical comment from the would-be matchmakers. "You've been spending too much time in the fast life to ever meet a really down-to-earth man you can care about." "How do you expect to meet a man if you're always hanging around the church?" "Forget the singles bars. There's this club I belong to, you know, the one where I met Rick? Well, he tells me that there are a lot of men just like him who are always hanging around and he wants you to be our guest . . ."

The introductions never take, of course, adding to the pain the woman endures. She experiences what, for her, is perceived as one more failure, one more disappointment.

Or she tries the matchmaking service of the decade, the classifieds. "Attractive SWF blonde (brunette, redhead), sophisticated, vivacious, world traveler, seeks mature, financially secure SWM to share travel, concerts, long walks in the moonlight, dancing, and romance. Possible long-term relationship? Contact Box. . . ."

Depending upon the area, the classifieds may actually provide what would be Mr. Right if the kept woman was not still at a stage where she felt the need to sabotage every relationship. Yet no matter what her luck with the classifieds, again there is failure.

Then the answer seems to be some sort of counseling. The woman locates a psychologist, psychiatrist, or religious counselor and complains about the emptiness in her life. She feels a failure regardless of her achievements and it becomes a matter of the therapist's skill, experience, and compassion as to whether or not the root cause will be found and erased.

On the other hand is the woman who becomes embittered. She "knows" that there is nothing wrong with her. Maybe men are no good. Maybe she is fated by the gods to be "dumped on." Maybe someone is deliberately out to get her. Maybe she is too good for the men in her city. Whatever her justification, there is an angry denial.

The embittered woman's life will take one of several different ends when she has left the kept life-style. Perhaps most common is the angry withdrawal from the social life that had been so normal for her. She can no longer be seen at the restaurants where she used to be a regular. She can no longer count upon spending the seasons in different parts of the world. If she retains any friendships, they are either with people who are no longer perceived as rivals or they are with new people who did not know her background. She may leave photographs and memorabilia on her walls and in scrapbooks. Or she may wipe out the evidence of her past, her surroundings, giving no clue to where she had been and the men she had known.

Other reactions occur as well. Some of the embittered seek same-sex relationships. They have been hurt by men for years. They have been manipulated and manipulators in return. Instead of recognizing that anyone can choose to do harm to another human being and that the problem has been with the type of relationships, not the sex, they give up on all men. They seek love and comfort from a "sister." The women are not lesbians but they will have same-sex experiences because of the pain.

Sometimes the same-sex relationships continue for many years. At other times the women realize that such relationships do not reflect their natural tendencies or desires. When this occurs, they may seek therapy or they may become asexual, avoiding intimacy with anyone. They may also become asexual when the same-sex relationship is with someone who is as emotionally abusive as the men she had known in the past. Some women realize that perhaps they have been wrong about men, that it is the quality of the individual and not the sex that matters. Others decide that everyone is no good and that the only comfort they will have is by being secure with themselves.

Motivation for Contacting a Therapist

Once a woman decides to seek therapy, the first step toward recovery is to recognize what has been wrong with the kept life-style. This is not necessarily the way she will enter therapy, however. Usually she will come for reasons that do not seem directly related. She may report health problems or other emotionally related illnesses that have not been found to have a specific organic cause. Or she may complain of depression, extreme tiredness, or some other difficulty. It is extremely rare that the woman will understand that having been a kept woman is the symptom of a deeper emotional problem.

There are several points that the kept woman must recognize when she first starts therapy.

1. A kept woman is usually angry, though this anger may have been so internalized that it is first seen as depression. And despite her claiming to friends and to herself that being kept provides a woman with the ultimate control over the man ("He does anything I want because he knows that if he doesn't, I'll leave him"), she knows that she is out of control. She must be at the man's beck and call if she wants to continue the relationship. There are certain, often unspoken, ground rules that she must obey. To do otherwise is to find herself without the apartment, the clothing, the nice restaurants, and whatever other benefits she has enjoyed.

The kept woman often tells herself lies. One woman explained that there was no one better at sex than she was and that was how she kept the man in line. Another claimed that her attraction was the denial of sex, that the lust a man had for her made him want to do anything to please her for a chance to take her to bed. Still another spoke of her great beauty and how men would vie for the chance to have her on their arms. Yet all these statements were belied by the fact that these women kept changing partners. There was no permanence in their lives. The men who could not live without them managed to go on to other relationships with ease. Their positions with the men were so precarious from day to day that, ultimately, they would do whatever the men wanted or quietly seek a different man to keep them before making a break.

2. To live as a kept woman is to maintain an existence that involves secrecy, deceit, and betrayal. Most kept women are involved with married men. The men are hurting their wives by their unfaithfulness. The men are also hurting the women they keep by their inability to commit. The men can never be trusted and the women they keep can never live a totally honest life. The kept woman is betraying the wife by perpetuating the kept relationship while the man is married. And seldom can anyone trust anyone else during the time that the involvement is taking place.

3. The kept woman is not admired in American society. The idea of having someone pay the bills, of not having to work, of having money, glamorous clothing, and the other perquisites of being kept is a fantasy

of both sexes. But the woman who is actually living that life-style is held in disdain. She is considered a home wrecker, a prostitute, a leech. No one understands the trauma of her childhood. No one understands her addiction. They see only someone willing to live off another person who is usually married and thus cheating on his wife.

The man who maintains a kept woman also does not respect her. She fantasizes that she has his love and respect because of the presents he buys and the terms of endearment he uses. But the truth is that she is a toy, a plaything, someone who can provide him with amusement, perhaps intelligent conversation, sex, and companionship when he wants it. He knows that she has been bought and can and will be purchased again by someone else. She is an expensive diversion, not someone he expects to see next to him in bed in five years. She may even be considered the ultimate, high-priced hooker, though he knows that she would be shattered if he ever admitted that that was how he perceived her.

As a kept woman I played the games we all play, trying to perpetuate the fantasy. I have joked with other kept women about how sexually skilled we are, how we can control a man with our bodies. I have bragged that I am "better" than the average woman, yet the conversation sounds more like the confused adolescent ramblings of girls first trying to understand their relationships with boys. It is not the mature analysis of a relationship that adults might share. Instead, it harks back to a time when teenagers fight over boyfriends and there is a sense of possessiveness which is not only false but has no place in any mature relationship.

4. A kept woman dare not have any true friends. Other women are always viewed as competition. To be vulnerable to another human being, to be open, caring, emotionally sharing, could result in being hurt. A man is the enemy and the prize, someone to be manipulated and won. Since the type of man who will play this game is emotionally unable to commit, there is no chance for a friendship to develop. And the man who refuses to play the game is not desired because he might force the kept woman to reexamine her life.

A woman is always competition. If she is the right age, appearance, and intelligence, then there is the fear that the "friend" will use her newfound knowledge of the other woman's current man to "steal" the current man in a kept woman's life. If the "friend" is considerably older, she may be held in disdain. "She would love to have what I have.

I know she's jealous of me. She had her time, but that time is long past. I am the woman men desire now and she cannot handle that fact" is the common thought process.

5. The kept woman is constantly torn between the desire to control a man and to destroy the relationship, a conflict that assures constant tension and unhappiness. Controlling the man makes her feel safe. She cannot be hurt by him so long as she is in charge. She can hold him in disdain as he plies her with luxury, desires her for sex, and generally behaves like a fawning sycophant. At the same time, if she does not destroy the relationship, there may come a moment when he is drawn to another woman. The idea of his leaving her is shattering, removing all her controls. Thus her sense of survival tells her to act first, leaving him. It is a constant conflict that keeps her perpetually insecure.

6. The kept woman lives the lie of independence. "I value my freedom too much to ever want to marry," said Ronnie. "A wife is nothing more than chattel. He's got this little nothing living out in the suburbs like someone on a 1950s television sitcom. It's like watching *Father Knows Best* or *Leave It to Beaver*. He gives the 'little woman' her allowance. He pats her on the head when dinner is ready. She goes to PTA and volunteers at the local hospital. The only difference between her and a pet dog is that she'll live longer.

"No man is going to do that to me. I'm independent. Always have been.

"Look at me. I've got a great job in real estate. I work whatever hours I want, coming and going as I please. I get taken to nice restaurants. I have a great apartment, an expensive car, nice trips. The sex is great, and when it's over, I can throw him out, get in the bathtub, and read a book while luxuriating in the hot water. I don't have to plan my life around some man and his wishes. Why would I want to marry?"

Yet how independent is Ronnie? "All right. So he pays for the apartment. But why shouldn't he? He wanted me to have a place near his office so he could drop over when he wanted, and you know how high the rents are here. If he wants me convenient, he can damn well pay for the privilege."

Then he expects you to be available to him?

"He calls the office first. I mean, I can't just drop everything because he wants a roll in the sack. I've got clients. Appointments. But I usually know his schedule and when he'll want to take a break, so it's no big deal to make certain I'm flexible during those hours."

What about traveling. Where do you go?

"Business trips. He has international dealings and he likes me to accompany him. Sometimes he takes his wife and I travel separately. Sometimes I go with him. It's a nice break from the office routine here."

He pays for your apartment. He pays for your trips. You make yourself available to him for sex. I don't see the independence.

"Then you're a fool. I told you. I'm not like his little Suzy Home-maker out in the suburbs. I'm an independent career woman with my own job, my own life, my own friends. That's what makes me better than her. That's why I have no intention of marrying."

It was a story repeated over and over again. The wife is a slave to the man's whims. The kept woman is independent, beholden to no one. Yet she is so frightened of losing the man's attention that she will do anything he desires. Ronnie greatly limited her real estate practice because she dared not show houses during the period when the businessman who kept her might want to drop by for sex. She was actually less free than a wife because she was constantly frightened of losing him if she failed to bring him pleasure.

7. The kept woman has a desire for traditional values yet is afraid that they don't exist. "What's a normal home?" asked Syl. "All I know is a father who's a drunk and a mother who walks all over him. That's how I was raised and I certainly don't think that I'm unique."

Most kept women come from backgrounds where the father was absent or uncaring. Their relationships have all been with men who are unable to emotionally commit. Usually the men are married, a subtle yet constant reminder that it is "normal" for men to cheat on their wives, emotionally abandon their families for other women.

The problem is compounded by the fact that the kept woman does not know where to meet a "normal" man. She is used to traveling in a social circle where the men routinely keep the women, separate their families from their pleasure, and involve themselves with those women who are comfortable with such a life-style. She will often seek a "normal" partner in what, for the majority of men, is an abnormal circumstance, then complain that all men are alike.

There is also little chance of the kept women's learning alternative ways to meet men from the few friends they may have. The women travel in the same social circles, know the same type of males, and have come to the same conclusions. The blind are leading the blind, yet all feel that they have special insight. They are unaware of how they have limited themselves.

Yet despite this problem, there is a constant nagging feeling that there can be something more to life. There is a desire for commitment on the part of both individuals. There may be a longing for children. Perhaps the kept woman wants to be at home, cooking, cleaning, and making the place desirable for the man who is out earning a living. Or she may want to be an independent person during the day, having a career, sharing the chores, constantly on the go except for weekends when they can enjoy a respite from the week, genuine intimacy, and perhaps an evening of entertainment. Whatever the circumstance, the kept woman wants to build memories with one man, knowing that they will share a lifetime together.

The conflict between what is desired and what she thinks she can actually attain causes great pain. Without awareness and the willingness to risk a different approach to living, the kept woman becomes a bitter cynic, miserable with life.

8. The kept woman never knows the real pain and peace of closure to a relationship. It is the nature of humans that we need to experience the feelings when relationships end. The rituals of death are almost entirely for the purpose of helping the living through the grief process. A similar grief process occurs with divorce or separation after a couple has lived together. There is a need to express pain, anger, joy, or whatever emotion is appropriate. There is a need to understand what has happened, to accept the fact that what was is now over and that the future will be quite different.

A kept woman does not have a clear break from each relationship. Her life is always in transition. While living with one man she may be planning her next move or fearing that the man will beat her to the ending of the relationship.

The kept woman's role is never clear because of the lack of commitment. The relationship is more a business transaction without a written contract than it is a love match. When it succeeds, the woman is never able to fully enjoy the role. When it fails, she is not able to finalize the end of the relationship. She has simply lost something that, in a sense, she has never had. The result is a constant uneasiness that can last for years.

Even a man's death does not provide a satisfactory closure. There are instances where the woman has been kept for several years, yet when the man becomes old, ill, unable to spend time with her without causing embarrassment to his family, she is again denied an ending. There usually is no way she can talk with him, put their lives in perspective, and prepare for going on alone. It does not matter whether or not he has arranged for her care after he has gone, though in the cases we studied, longer-term relationships always had some sort of annuity or "severance pay" benefit. The wife has the chance to work through the death, to spend the time with her husband that is needed to help serve as part of the closure when it is over. The kept woman lacks this contact and the pain lingers indefinitely.

9. The kept woman must recognize that even though she has never perceived love while growing up, she is, indeed, lovable. This is one of the most difficult things for any adult victim of child abuse to accept. In fact, few kept women enter therapy fully believing this. But, however difficult it is, they must at least recognize the possibility of it.

We want to believe the statement that home is the place you can always go when nobody else will have you. We think that a parent will love a child no matter what. We glorify parenting, glossing over the given that to be a parent all that is necessary is for a man and woman to have sex. And biology has nothing to do with providing emotional stability. The couple may not want a child. They may be unfit to raise another life. They may not even recognize what is involved with having a child.

Many people, including social workers, schoolteachers, and others, often do not wish to acknowledge that being a loving, nurturing parent takes more skill than just having a baby. They do not get involved so long as dysfunctional families are keeping their problems within the confines of their own homes. The child who is neglected, emotionally abused, or even physically abused in ways that do not leave obvious marks, will often go unnoticed. There is no one to alter the child's perspective that he or she is lacking in self-worth.

Once a child who has been denied love reaches adulthood, he or she has a sense of being unique. The adult has become so accustomed to hiding the abuse that occurred during childhood that he or she is uncomfortable discussing it.

The kept woman who lacks a sense of self-worth is constantly frightened that she will be unmasked as a fraud. She knows that she is dominating men, letting them buy her gifts and vie for her favors.

She also knows that if they ever perceive what she believes is the truth about herself, she will be humiliated.

It takes great courage to accept the fact that not only was love not received as a child but also that that is not a reflection on the woman herself. She has to expose herself to the therapist who to her mind just might find that she is as bad as she fears herself to be. Everything might be fine or it might not and there is no way to know except to risk all future self-esteem. Yet this is what the kept woman must do to get help.

Admitting to the Problem

A major step is admitting to the problem, both to oneself and to others. We kept women have a great many denial mechanisms we call upon.

For example, one of my approaches has been to try and establish a group of current and former kept women who can meet on a regular basis to discuss mutual problems. I have frequently said that I gain more from the group than I gain from therapy, yet when my coauthor interviewed some of the women involved with the group, he found their impressions were not always the same as mine. He also found women throughout the country who have tried group self-help as well as therapy and their statements caused me to question myself.

The truth is that my approach may have been and may continue to be another form of denial. I know that I am addicted to the kept-woman life-style. It is healthy to admit this to and discuss it with women who instantly recognize a sister in pain, a woman who is unsure of herself, desperate for approval, and willing to do anything to gain the approval of a man who will never commit to a relationship. A conversation within a group of women who are experiencing the same addiction should be helpful. The question I have to ask myself, as others are asking themselves in different parts of the country where this is being tried, is whether or not I started the group to avoid facing my problem. If I am the guide who encourages conversation, the sympathetic, understanding listener, might I not also be setting myself up to avoid openly talking about my own problems? The truth is that those of us in a leadership role may use that role to be less vulnerable, to avoid talking about our innermost fears and sorrows.

Equally bad is the fact that we are the blind leading the blind. We all know the same type of men. We all have shared the same types of relationships. We all have used similar defense mechanisms and come to similar conclusions about our lives. We have no idea what is "normal." We support each other's pain, yet I wonder how well we are able to help each other move forward since we have never known any alternatives. That is why the majority of women we interviewed felt that the greatest assistance comes from working with a professional therapist, not a self-help group.

Yet everything starts with admitting that we have a problem. Without that, nothing can be accomplished.

The last two steps follow quickly. Once you admit to the problem, it is much easier to learn about the condition and then enter therapy. Like any addiction, the kept-woman addiction can be overcome, though the results are sometimes surprising.

The Difficulty in Change

Dr. Shulman and other therapists talked about the problems many kept women have in recognizing that they can change their lives. The fortunate ones have held a job for a number of years, have marketable skills, and/or enough money to be able to support themselves without being kept. The majority of the women feel helpless, having been out of the marketplace for many years, perhaps without savings or assets convertible to cash. Many of us purchase clothing and cosmetics because how we look is so important, never considering that we might need something else. We may be destitute or qualified for low-paying jobs by the time we seek help.

The first concern for the therapist is often trying to make us feel better about ourselves. We feel that our lives are over. We feel that we cannot relate to the majority of women who are coping very well in circumstances that may actually be far worse than our own.

"I get my patients walking," explained Dr. Shulman. "I have them take a brisk, aerobic walk for at least a half an hour a day between sessions.

"There is no way you can go for a long, aerobic walk, one that gets the blood circulating and your breathing going, without feeling better. Then, when they come back for their next session, I ask them how they felt after they finished with their walk each day. They always tell me that they feel much better. They sometimes are surprised by how much better they feel.

"That is the first step. Once they realize that just so simple an exercise as going for a walk can make them feel better, they can accept the fact that change might be possible in their lives. And once they accept the fact that they can change, they are ready to respond to therapy."

None of us wants to change, of course. We have been living a life of denial with just enough positive experiences so that we can reinforce the denial mechanism.

No matter how much sharing a couple may have, most women still have certain feelings that are carryovers from the days when men were supposed to be the sole provider. We were rated as wives by the gifts our men gave us. "He bought you a new mink coat (or car or boat or whatever)? Then he must really love you." "He's taking you to Europe? I can't get my Harry to take me for a weekend to see my sister Sarah. I'd love to have a man who cares for me like yours does." "You must be very special to him. Look at all he gives you." "How I envy the way you're treated."

There is a corollary to that type of thought process. It says that the woman who is not given the gifts, the vacations, and so on is not loved. She is not special to her husband. Never mind that the man might adore her but simply lack the earning capacity to provide such luxury. A woman who lacks "things" is a woman who believes herself to not be loved and respected by the man in her life.

Suddenly the kept woman has to learn a whole new set of rules for this game of life. She must learn to take pride in herself, in her self-sufficiency, in her ability to cope on her own. She must recognize that, in a sense, she was a user and that the kept-woman life-style had little to do with love or respect.

Then the kept woman must recognize that not having a relationship is preferable to having a destructive one. The only relationships that matter are those that involve commitment and mutual support. Such relationships can be found but not among the men with whom she has been involved. She can have everything she desires in life if she is willing to stand on her own.

Eventually, though, what matters is her effort on her own behalf. For example, I took a job in the cosmetics field because it paid well enough for me to meet my expenses. I hated the job. I hated dealing with the public. I was doing things I never thought I could tolerate and I certainly did not enjoy the work. Yet each time I refused to travel with a man who called, each time I stayed home instead of going to parties where my only thought would be the "competition," I felt that I had made a personal triumph. After a year and a half of this, I was strong enough to begin considering what else I might want to do, what other type of work I wished to explore, what additional education I might desire to go in the direction that would be right for me.

Others found different approaches. "I went back to school," said Lenore. "I knew this guy who had kept me once and I went to him to borrow the money. I was still playing the manipulator and I knew it, but I didn't care. It was the last time and he was so rich that he could afford it even if I didn't pay him back.

"I just took courses. I bought a lot of dumpy clothes, stopped wearing makeup, and only made certain that I was neat and clean. I wore my eyeglasses instead of contacts and avoided focusing on my figure or my looks. I didn't want any reaction to my body. I wanted to blend in with the other students, some of whom were older than me, much to my surprise.

"I had no direction and didn't care. I spent all my free time either studying in the library or hanging out in the student union, reading, thinking, talking with the students.

"I listened to the eager young ones planning for a future they could not really anticipate. I talked with the older ones who were changing careers or trying to get the training they needed to advance. I discovered that I could have fun with people who were not trying to be the movers and shakers of the world. I talked with people who didn't care what I wore or what I owned. I found some kids who had traveled widely because of whatever it was their parents did and was surprised to find that they knew more about the countries we both had visited than I did. I knew the resorts, the beaches, the parties. They knew the people, the culture, the life-styles I had never seen, never considered wanting to know, and what they were talking about was far more interesting than anything I had known.

"I still don't know what I want to do with the rest of my life. I'm still terrified of being alone. But I'm looking for work now, if only on a part-time basis. And I recognize how shallow I've been, how shallow the so-called great leaders actually were. My life feels better for it."

Hang-ups from the Past

There are a number of carryovers for the kept woman. Some affect her therapy. Others will literally stay with her for many years and, probably, the rest of her life.

The most common minor problem is the inability to tell family secrets. All through childhood the typical kept woman thought that the abuse she suffered was either commonly experienced by others or unique. Either way she saw no reason to discuss it.

In most instances where the abuse took place, the kept woman was also warned that to discuss "family business" was wrong. There were secrets to be kept, things that were not to be made public. Maybe Daddy was "tired a lot," a euphemism for a drinking problem that caused him to batter his family and pass out on the floor. Perhaps there was a "funny" uncle who liked to show his affection by touching the wrong parts of the body. No matter what the problem, the kept woman was taught in childhood that it was wrong to reveal the information. It was a betrayal that must never occur.

Fortunately once the kept woman has initiated the four steps described in this chapter, she intellectually is aware that it is all right to talk about the past. She will still feel guilty, but at least she knows that *feeling* guilty is not the same as *being* guilty. More important, once she begins talking, the act of discussing such matters sets her free. Each revelation makes the next problem easier to discuss until she realizes that keeping the problems inside was destructive. She was the innocent victim and there is nothing wrong with revealing the truth.

More insidious is what has been found to occur in the intimate lives of the recovered kept women. The typical kept woman has been conditioned to tolerate pain and inappropriate behavior. In many instances she is like the woman who has become involved with white slavery against her will. She has been battered emotionally and physically until she not only can tolerate that which was once intolerable, she often cannot get pleasure except through some variation of what she was taught by the men who kept her.

Naomi, for example, spent fifteen years in the Washington, D.C., area being kept by a number of major political leaders. She was eighteen, a new secretary, having trouble with an abusive father and an alcoholic mother, when she was approached by a senator. He was young, in his early thirties, and considered a rising star in Washington.

He wanted to take her to dinner, to thank her for her efforts with his committee, to get to know her better.

The senator was a perfect gentleman the entire time they dined together. Naomi knew that he was married, but the fact that he never tried to touch her, that he kept the conversation about her and her plans for the future, convinced her that his interest was strictly professional.

There were other meals together in the next few weeks. He began talking about forthcoming legislation that she knew about from her typing chores. He asked her opinion and took her responses seriously. She felt special, respected, and saw nothing unusual when, shortly after she turned nineteen, she was asked to join his personal staff at a substantial raise. She had no idea that she was being set up for something more personal.

"The first time he kissed me was when we learned that a bill he had sponsored had passed. I had done some minor work with the research behind it, though he gave me the impression that my role was far more important than it really was. Anyway, we were alone in his office, with the door closed, when he got word that it had passed. He leapt up, grabbed me, and kissed me.

"I was flustered and embarrassed, uncertain what to do. Don't get me wrong. I liked it. I liked the closeness and the pride he seemed to have in what we had accomplished together. But I wondered what I'd do if there was anything more. I wondered how I should act. I didn't realize that it was all a plan that had worked before with other girls and that he would do nothing else. There was the one kiss, the lingering touch of his hands in mine, the intense gaze into my eyes, the radiating of pure happiness, and then we went back to work.

"That night I felt as though I really mattered to someone for the first time in my life. I'd have done anything for him."

It was two more weeks before the senator made his move. The two of them worked late, dined, went back to the office, then continued working. Finally, close to midnight, she asked if his wife wouldn't miss him if he didn't go home soon. She didn't realize that his wife was out of town visiting her family and he didn't tell her. Instead he explained that they were not getting along very well, that they had been leading separate lives, that they would be divorcing after the next election.

"He told me that his wife knew the voters would be angry about his getting a divorce. He said that she believed in him and his work even though they no longer loved each other, no longer even shared the same bedroom. She would not do anything to hurt his chance for reelection and she told him that by the time he completed six years as a bachelor senator in his next term, the voters wouldn't care if he was married or not.

"It all sounded so logical and I felt so sorry for this brilliant, lonely man who I knew was making the world a better place in which to live. God, I was naïve.

"Anyway, we worked another hour or two, then he kissed me good night, saying he was going to sleep in the office because home only brought him bad memories. He kissed me again, this time with some passion to it, and I left that office wanting him like I had never wanted anyone else. We became lovers before the week was out."

The senator kept Naomi on the payroll but arranged for her to have an apartment near the office where they could escape whenever they had some free time for sex. Then, just as smoothly as he had seduced her, he introduced her to a rougher kind of lovemaking.

"He was very clever about it, just as he had been about kissing me that first time. I had made some stupid mistake and he swatted my ass. I yelped and he said something like I had been a bad little girl and should be spanked. Then he got this mischievous grin on his face, put me over his knee, and lightly spanked me. It seemed all in fun, but he got an intense hard-on. His face was flushed and his breathing was ragged. When I started to get up, he pulled down his zipper and made it very clear that he wanted oral sex.

"I wasn't thrilled with the idea, but by this time I loved him and would do anything for him. I almost choked and he went back to straight sex for a while before repeating the incident. This time the oral sex was a little easier for me, though I was bothered by the fact that he seemed to get more pleasure from it than when we did it straight.

"One thing led to another until he stopped by my apartment with some handcuffs. I wanted to know what they were and he said he got them from an FBI agent friend. Naïvely I believed him and let him take me 'prisoner' and handcuff me to the bedposts. He spanked me again, this time harder. Then he freed my wrists, handcuffing them again behind my back before having me give him oral sex.

"I didn't like what he was doing, yet he really wasn't hurting me. I figured he was going through some childish phase or something and didn't question as much as I should have. I figured he worked hard and if this sort of thing brought him pleasure, it was no big deal."

The sex became rougher. The senator introduced a variety of gadgets to the sex act, seeming to get his pleasure from what he could do to Naomi, not with her. Then, a few weeks before she gained the courage to walk out on him, he introduced another woman into the sex play and she realized that she was not the focus of his interests. He liked sadomasochistic activities and the woman involved did not really matter.

"By this time there was nothing I wouldn't let him do with me. He had one of those leather ball gag things, handcuffs, some sort of soft whip that was a little like being stung by a feather boa, and a vibrator he liked using more than having me himself. He was always so gentle, so kind, so attentive and loving during all other phases of our relationship that I closed my eyes to what else was going on. It was only when he wanted another woman and had the nerve to bring her in when I was naked and helpless that I realized what a real piece of shit he was."

But walking out on the senator was not the end of it. Naomi had met a number of powerful government figures, lobbyists, military leaders, congressmen, and so forth through the senator. One of them, a former general who was involved with a big defense contractor, asked her for a date. He told her that he had always been interested in her ever since the senator had told him so much about her, only he had never asked her out because he knew that she was the senator's private property.

"There was much more involved than I realized at the time. These guys had like a network for their S&M stuff. Over the years I saw the pattern where the same women would be at the same parties, only periodically the men they were with would change. They would be with one man for a few months, then go with another, always in this same circle. And always we were given an apartment, clothes, an allowance. Some of us worked. Others were just kept. But what they had done was find women who would tolerate a sadomasochistic relationship."

Eventually Naomi found that she psychologically prepared herself for sex with a degree of violence. She found that she so anticipated the abuse that she had difficulty lubricating when the man wanted straight sex. It was not that she enjoyed the pain. It was a case of conditioning, a little like what happens with people who have been held hostage for a prolonged period of time. An extreme example of which was the California case where a woman was kidnapped while hitchhiking, then kept bound, gagged, and trapped in a box for weeks, removed only so she could eat, take care of her bodily functions, and be raped. She eventually became so psychologically defeated and at the same time determined to do whatever she needed to do to stay alive that she went along with whatever the man and his wife desired. For seven years, before being discovered by a neighbor, she worked in their house, acted as a sex slave, and made no effort to escape when she had the chance to go free. She made what she felt was the necessary adjustment, never realizing that she was giving herself long-term psychological damage in the process.

The same was true with Naomi. She became so used to the abusive behavior that, though she did not wish it, she also found that she needed a certain amount of abusive stimulation to relax and be ready for intercourse. This was especially a problem when she met Tom, a lawyer who was single, not abusive, and very much in love with her.

"By this time I had been in counseling and knew that what I was experiencing was not unusual. I convinced Tom to come with me to the therapist's and she explained the situation to both of us. She said that many victims of abusive sex as children or those who experience such things when they first become sexually active have the same problem. She said that the answer was to work out ways to enjoy sex that were modifications we could both enjoy. We had to find something that would give me pleasure and not be repugnant to Tom, who could never imagine striking me for any reason. He loved me too much to want anything but pleasure for me."

There are many ways that the problems are resolved, according to the therapists, though the change is often different than some people expect. Instead of being able to change the subconscious programming completely, most therapists find that a kept woman who has become accustomed to abuse, to tolerating the intolerable, will change only to a limited degree.

"I find that I need to get the man in her life to accept the slightly unconventional so that the kept woman who has entered into a healthy relationship can retain just enough from the past to be comfortable," said a Miami, Florida, therapist who asked to remain anonymous. His client list includes women who have been kept by a number of major Northern industrialists who maintain business offices, retirement houses, or second houses in the Miami and Miami Beach areas.

"For example, I had this one woman who was involved with a series of rock musicians who liked to get her high on drugs, then engage in sadomasochistic sex. There were two problems she faced, the chemical dependency and the conditioning to feel comfortable with sex only when she was restricted in some way. There was a period in her life of a couple of years when she was kept by one rock star who paid her extremely well, surrounded her with luxury, but kept her handcuffed or chained to the bed at night, engaging in a variety of sex acts at any time he felt like it. She became so accustomed to his abnormal tastes that it took her several months after she left him to be comfortable sleeping more than a couple of hours at a time and to be comfortable sleeping without her hands being restricted.

"A lot of my fellow therapists with whom I have discussed this think that it is our job to return her to the same conditioning the average woman has in a normal relationship. But I think that this is asking too much and may not be realistic when you consider the psychological conditioning she has already endured. What I find is that it is easiest to counsel with both the woman and the man in her life with whom she is having a committed relationship after she is out of the kept life.

"The woman who had been with the rock star found the ideal answer in experiencing bondage with her new partner. They bought several long scarves which he used to tie and gag her as part of their foreplay. He makes certain she is restricted enough so she feels she cannot get loose, yet comfortable enough so that there is no pain. Then he touches her body, kissing and caressing her. Sometimes she wants him to tell her she has been a bad girl and that she is not going to be able to leave the room until he is done with her. And she admits that she sometimes fantasizes that he will spank her if she tries to get loose from the bonds. But the man loves her too much to ever consider actually causing her any pain. He understands her past, understands her need for the bondage, and has learned to enjoy a type of relationship he never thought about experiencing.

"My patient once told me something interesting about the experience. She said that with S&M, a person is restricted in order to feel pain. With bondage, the person is restricted in order to feel pleasure. I see nothing unhealthy about that way of thinking. In fact, with bondage without pain being a popular form of sex play among people comfortable with many variations of nonabusive sex, the compromise in the relationship seems to put the couple into a normal situation. I also think that she will come to want a relationship where she does not always feel the need to be restricted in some manner. But even if she doesn't, she is getting married to a good man, they are happy, and she is no longer afraid of commitment. I consider that to be healthy."

Other therapists have found variations of what the Miami doctor described. One psychiatrist said that one of his patients, a formerly kept woman, was always verbally abused before sex. She still likes the man to do this, though not meaning the words as the men in her past meant them. She becomes excited when her new husband laughingly calls her a "bitch" or a "cunt" during the sex act. They are words he would never have called her without her request and he does not think of her in so derogatory a manner as did the men in her past, but his using them has enabled her to make a transition in the way she thinks.

The therapists stressed that the problems the kept woman may face during sex are not so extreme as they may sound, though. During a normal, healthy relationship, a man and a woman may call each other names, engage in bondage, light spanking, wrestling, or almost anything else. They may engage in oral sex. They may combine intercourse with manual stimulation, either by hand or with a vibrator. They may do any one of dozens of different actions all meant to give the other person pleasure. The difference is that the abused kept woman is going from violent actions to nonviolent variations from traditional sex. The woman who has not experienced such painful conditioning in her past is going from fairly simple mutual pleasuring, such as the missionary position following what may be fairly brief foreplay, to extended foreplay with whatever method for achieving orgasm the couple mutually enjoys.

There are other problems as well. The formerly kept woman may feel insecure and need to be certain that the man will not suddenly abandon her. She may need reassurance, if only in the form of understanding of what she is going through. In a healthy relationship the man may look at another woman and comment on her overall beauty or some unusually attractive feature of her body or personality, knowing his wife or girlfriend will not be jealous. The man involved with the formerly kept woman is going to experience the same pleasure in seeing another woman but he will have to explain himself more fully. He may find that to reassure the woman he is with he needs to say something to the effect of: "I certainly like the way that woman looks when she walks. She's almost as attractive as you are. It's too bad she doesn't have your personality. Then she'd really be beautiful in the ways that truly matter."

The degree to which the kept woman may fully recover is determined by how long she has been kept and how abusive the relationships have been. Just as the woman with a mildly abusive childhood may enter a kept relationship that lasts for years because she is less insecure about herself than the woman who has been able to stay in relationships only for weeks or months at a time, so the recovery is dependent upon the history of the kept relationship. Yet all kept women can learn to commit emotionally through therapy. The other aftereffects can be resolved satisfactorily between the woman and the man with whom she becomes involved.

The other problem many kept women face during recovery is actually quite similar to what housewives with grown children experience when returning to the marketplace. This is the inability to respect their own achievements and to analyze their skills.

"I know which knives and forks to use when eating," said Ellie. "I know how to dress when going to an affair with a head of state. I know which shoes to wear on a yacht. But I can't type. I can't take dictation. And I've certainly never run my own business."

Sometimes the women are in as bad a situation as Ellie claimed she was in. They entered the kept life-style right out of high school and never trained for anything. Yet usually the women have developed what they consider to be hobbies—photography, modeling, acting, painting, cooking, or any number of other things. Valerie was sent to the Cordon Bleu school to learn to cook by a politician who wanted her to oversee parties he held while keeping her. She understood food preparation, the decorating of plates and tables, and how to handle complex menus for one person or a hundred. Yet she never thought about that as a marketable skill until her therapist convinced her to start talking with restaurant owners and hotel managers. She is now making sixty-five thousand dollars a year working for a Chicago restaurant and is delighted by her feeling of independence.

Linda was an artist who bragged that she had sold everything she ever painted. However, she deliberately limited her artwork because she feared that she might not be respected for it. She also knew that while she was competent, she needed more training to become commercial enough to truly earn a living at what she enjoyed.

After therapy Linda went into partnership in an art gallery and auction house. She sells the work of artists whose paintings command prices of a thousand to fifty thousand dollars each and auctions work of much greater value. She has returned actively to painting, selling her own work through other galleries since it is not yet up to the standards demanded by her clientele. However, she has begun taking lessons with one of the more successful fine artists her gallery represents so that she can improve her technique and see how far she can advance. She is no longer afraid of rejection, ridicule, or independence.

Several therapists have sent formerly kept women to career counselors where they learn to evaluate the skills they previously did not respect. One woman who truly had no skills became extremely successful in the sales field. She discovered that the ability to read the reactions of the men and women with whom she interacted when she was being kept would enable her to be successful selling. There are formerly kept women working in fashion divisions of department stores, handling display advertising sales for newspapers and magazines, selling air time for radio and television, and any number of other items in expensive specialty stores. They have learned to judge quality, know the type of people who are able to buy the products, and speak their language.

11

Tomorrow

A s I look back on my life as a kept woman, and as I reflect on the experiences of other kept women, I have come to understand so many things. For example, the most difficult lesson to learn is that behavior that is appropriate for one period of our lives may be destructive during another time.

I was born to a mother who was little more than a child herself; I was unable to understand her constant battle for survival as someone who was a teenage bride, teenage mother, and uneducated for any meaningful job in the marketplace. The boy that she married was an irresponsible alcoholic who was abusive and a probable incest victim. There was no way that we children could experience the nurturing that we desired. There was no way that we could experience the support that we wanted because keeping us alive was the greatest challenge she faced, the only challenge she could handle.

It was necessary for me to establish a fantasy life revolving around my absent father. I became Cinderella, only the wicked Stepmother was my real mother and the handsome Prince was the immature, alcoholic boy who abandoned us. I came to see the buying of presents, the secret rendezvous, the occasional surprise of being carried off to a magical place as the ultimate giving of love.

My fantasies carried me through my childhood, just as the fantasies of the women we interviewed carried them through theirs. What I did not know, did not understand, was that carrying them into adult relationships would prove destructive. They reinforced my seeming weakness, my lack of a sense of self-worth. They led me into a destructive fantasy game that could end only in emotional tragedy.

I never wanted to get out of the kept life-style. It was the only way I knew to live, the only way I knew to keep score of whether or not I was winning in the game of life. And there are still bitter moments when I wonder why I bothered to try and survive the abrupt way I was forced to face myself, my past, and my future.

Recognizing that I was not alone helped, of course. I came to see that much of my background was shared to some degree by others. Their attitudes might be different. Their experiences might be far more pleasurable or far more destructive than what I both sought and endured. But we were still "sisters" in a world the average man or woman knows nothing about.

I tried many ways to recover. I abstained from sex. I abstained from male relationships. I formed my own group-therapy sessions and I sought personal counseling as well.

Sometimes it seemed as though I was taking two steps forward and three steps backward. At other times I was making progress that could be measured in inches when I knew that I had miles to go. But at least the inches were moving in a positive direction and that was something new in my life.

I explored different spiritual paths, becoming involved with both Christianity and metaphysics, a natural combination for me, a seeming contradiction to others. Yet the reactions of others no longer mattered so much to me. I was searching, trying to find answers, directions, a reason to go on with life.

I became involved with a man who was not rich, who could not take me to the most expensive restaurants, fly me around the world, or even pay for taxis in which I could travel. I remained uncomfortable with the physical aspects of the relationship, preferring to think of the two of us as sharing something spiritual. Yet I found that I could at least think about sex, not considering it necessarily painful, dirty, violent, or evil. I recognized that it could be an expression of love in a manner that just might be more intense and pleasurable than any other action between a man and a woman.

Eventually I decided to write this book. I wanted to understand my own life and the lives of others like me. I knew that without the purpose and direction that this book could provide, I would never have the nerve to explore this phenomenon that is at once so fascinating, glamorous, and deadly.

I was surprised by much of what I learned, both about myself and others. I had to confront the fact that I had never tried to understand my mother and that my rejection of her resulted in her not being able to understand my life. I recognized that my father was sick and vicious, the most negative role model I had encountered during my formative years. And I learned that it is all right for me to stand on my own two feet, to go to work, to draw a paycheck, to live in surroundings that I can afford, whatever that means.

I am still troubled. I am still uneasy when someone wants to discuss my past and the lives of others like me. I still cringe when I hear someone say that the life I led is glamorous, the ultimate fantasy a woman could enjoy.

Yet I know that with each day I am getting stronger. I am broadening my range of acquaintances. I am exploring the first healthy relationship with a male I have ever had in my adult life.

I am an addict in every sense of that word as it is applied to alcoholics, drug users, and other kinds of addicts. Yet like the addict who recognizes his or her addiction and seeks to stop it one day at a time, I am getting stronger and healthier, becoming the woman I know I can be.

I have also found that accepting God has helped me tremendously. By loving the Creator, I can learn to love and accept His creation. Church involvement and an effort to understand the teachings of Jesus have been extremely important to me. They also provide an ongoing support when I become frightened of ongoing desires that I know would be destructive if acted upon.

I have a ways to go. I am constantly struggling, constantly praying, constantly doing battle with my emotions. Yet like so many of the other women in this book who are overcoming the life-style few ever have the opportunity to know, I am going to make it.

APPENDIX

If you are a kept woman, have been one, or just come from a dysfunctional family and recognize aspects of your own personality you realize you need to change, there are a number of counselors and groups that may be of help.

The first choice is usually private counseling. However, therapists vary in skill, quality, and understanding, regardless of their training. Talk with the therapist first, explaining a little of your problem, and see if you are comfortable. If not, try a different therapist. You will almost certainly have to pay for these sessions, but that is a smaller price than the cost of therapy with someone you do not feel is helpful.

Therapists can be obtained through referrals by friends, doctors, mental health centers, family counseling agencies, or your county psychological and psychiatric associations. There may also be help lines or crisis lines in your community that can provide such services.

Group help is available from a number of programs modeled after Alcoholics Anonymous. These are generally twelve-step programs involving individuals similar to yourself who get together to work their way through the shared difficulties they face. Not all groups meet in all communities, though most will be found in large cities. Also, groups vary even though the concepts are the same. You may find yourself compatible with the people and their approach in one group and uncomfortable with another. Again, do not be afraid to change.

The groups are usually listed in the telephone book. If not, call those that are, such as Alcoholics Anonymous. Crisis counseling centers, help lines, and the various associations mentioned below may also be able to refer you. Among the most commonly utilized by adults who have shared the experiences in this book are the following:

Adult Children of Alcoholics	Debtors Anonymous
Adult Children Anonymous	Emotions Anonymous
Alcoholics Anonymous	Parents Anonymous
Al-Anon	Pills Anonymous
Bulimics/Anorexics Anonymous	Sexaholics Anonymous
Child Abusers Anonymous	Sex Addicts Anonymous
Cocaine-Anonymous	Sex and Love Addicts Anonymous
Co-dependents of Sex Addicts	

Most of these groups will welcome you freely. The sex-addicts type of group may use some screening procedures to protect the members. The problems are serious but the concept sounds titillating. The members try to protect themselves from the curious, but they will welcome anyone with a serious problem.

There may be other groups offering similar help. The ones I've listed are those most commonly found throughout the United States. They are all based on the twelve-step program AA has found so workable over the years.

From a personal perspective, I have found that finding a religious group with which I feel compatible is important for my healing. Whether this is Jewish or Christian does not matter. The particular denomination does not matter. It is the knowledge and love of God that is important, so you may need to try several groups before you find one with which you feel comfortable. What matters is the acceptance of His love as you understand it, and the growth and support that comes from a church or synagogue where you feel both welcome and uplifted.